MIGRATION AND DEVELOPMENT IN AFRICA: AN OVERVIEW

Richard Black, Jonathan Crush, Sally Peberdy with
Savina Ammassari, Lyndsay McLean Hilker,
Shannon Mouillesseaux, Claire Pooley, Radha Rajkotia

African Migration and Development Series No. 1

ACKNOWLEDGEMENTS

This publication is the product of a collaboration between the Southern African Migration Project and the Development Research Centre on Migration, Globalisation and Poverty at Sussex University. The authors would like to thank all those contacted during the course of research for this paper for their helpful suggestions and comments. Elizabeth Jones and Bridget Dillon at DFID were particularly helpful, as was the Migration Team at DFID. The original set of papers on which this publication is based was funded by DFID as part of a broader 2003 scoping exercise on the relationship between migration and pro-poor development policy. Responsibility for the views expressed remains with the authors.

Published by Idasa, 6 Spin Street, Church Square, Cape Town, 8001, and Queen's University, Canada.

© Southern African Migration Project (SAMP) 2006
ISBN 1-920118-16-0

First published 2006
Produced by Idasa Publishing

CONTENTS

TABLES

Chapter 1

MIGRATION, POVERTY & DEVELOPMENT IN AFRICA

1.1 Overview

Migration is clearly a major issue across Africa. Indeed, migration – both within countries and across borders – can be seen as an integral part of labour markets and livelihoods across much of the continent for at least the last century. Over time, and in different places, migration has taken a number of different forms. It has cut across class and skill boundaries, and exists in widely different geographical and demographic contexts. Migration represents an important livelihood strategy for poor households seeking to diversify their sources of income, but is also characteristic of the better off, and indeed of many African elites.

In practice, however, the link between migration and poverty is often viewed more negatively. It is assumed across much of the continent that it is poverty that forces poor people to migrate, rather than migration being a potential route out of poverty. The poor are also generally seen as those worst affected by conflict-induced migration, itself a prominent feature in Africa. The movement of skilled and/or wealthy Africans is also generally viewed negatively (e.g. there is long-standing concern on the African continent with the impact of the 'brain drain' of African professionals). Only slowly, and in relatively few quarters, is understanding emerging of the potentially positive role that migration itself can play in reducing poverty, or of the possibilities for 'mobilisation' of the African diaspora in the fight against poverty. Meanwhile, public policy remains a long way from building effectively on such understanding.

The aim of this study is to synthesise existing research on migration in Africa, and its relationship to development policy. The report focuses on the relationship between migration, poverty and pro-poor development policy. Pro-poor policy is taken here to mean policies that are context-specific, listen and react to poor people's voices, and/or seek to assist poor people to become less vulnerable and build up their income and assets. Government health and education policies might not be considered intrinsically pro-poor, but become so where they are targeted at widening access to health and education services, and especially basic health and education services (e.g. primary care, vaccination campaigns, primary schooling), or at responding to the specific needs of the poor. Pro-poor policies might also seek to identify and support poor people's livelihoods, through the promotion of social protection mechanisms (ranging from pensions, health insurance, maternity benefit and unemployment benefits to food aid and other social assistance) or enhancement and enforcement of poor people's rights. In turn, our focus is not only on the policies of developing country governments, but also on those of non-government and intergovernmental organisations, and of donor nations. In terms of migration, the study covers both international and internal migration.

In the sections that follow, issues are dealt with first in relation to sub-Saharan Africa as a whole, and then in detail for three regions – West Africa, East Africa and Southern Africa. The sections on Africa as a whole, and on West and East Africa were completed by researchers at the Sussex Centre for Migration Research at the University of Sussex, whilst the section on Southern Africa was written by researchers at the Southern African Migration Project.

1.2 General Findings

- Migration can be seen as an integral part of labour markets and livelihoods across much of the African continent for at least the last century. Over time, and in different places, it has taken a number of different forms. It has included internal, regional and international movements. It has cut across class and skill boundaries, and exists in widely different demographic contexts. Migration represents an important livelihood strategy for poor households seeking to diversify their sources of income, but is also characteristic of the better off, and indeed of many African elites.

- There are estimated to be between 20 and 50 million migrants in Africa, although statistical data on migration flows are incomplete and often outdated, and there are significant undocumented flows. The most important countries of immigration are Côte d'Ivoire and South Africa, whilst Somalia, Eritrea, Ethiopia, Ghana, Senegal, Cape Verde, Liberia, Sierra

Leone, Mali, Gambia, Zimbabwe and South Africa are all significant countries of emigration.

- Internal migration involves men, women and children, and includes rural-rural, urban-rural and urban-urban flows as well as rural-urban movements. Links between rural and urban areas developed by migration are significant in promoting remittances, encouraging community level initiatives for the construction of public facilities and infrastructure, and linking rural producers to urban markets.

- Although evidence is patchy, patterns of internal migration appear to have been affected by economic crisis and structural adjustment, with some arguing that a long trend of urbanisation across the continent has been stopped or even reversed, sometimes with negative effects on rural livelihoods.

- Migration to Europe and the United States is predominantly of educated individuals, giving rise to considerable concern over the issue of 'brain drain'. However, once again data is incomplete, and some claims may be exaggerated. International migrants also appear to remit significant amounts of money to Africa, through both formal and informal channels.

- Sub-Saharan Africa has witnessed significant flows of forced migrants, including internally displaced people and victims of trafficking. However, peace processes in a number of African countries suggest attention needs to be turned urgently towards facilitating sustainable return.

- Occupational diversification in rural areas is often inextricably linked to mobility, whilst migration has been a key factor in shaping settlement patterns and livelihoods. One recent study by IIED found that a staggering 50-80 per cent of rural households had at least one migrant member, across all wealth categories, and with increasing involvement of women as independent migrants. However, the study also found that remittances had declined over a 15-year period, largely as a result of employment insecurity in destination areas, even though at the same time rural households had become more dependent on these remittances.

- Eleven countries are signatories to the Migrant Workers' Convention – more than in any other world region. The ILO has designed and launched an 'African Labour Migration Policy Initiative' which seeks to enhance the knowledge base on labour migration and build capacity of labour ministries and others to deal with labour migration.

- In relation to the brain drain, there is particular concern about the impacts on health of migration of doctors and nurses. The impact of migration on health outcomes for poor people is felt not only through migration of health personnel to northern countries, but also through regional migration flows (e.g. to South Africa, Namibia and elsewhere), rural-urban migration within countries, and through 'migration' from the public to the private sector. However, policy in this sector needs to recognise the need of health professionals to gain skills and career enhancement through short-term mobility.

- Despite emerging interest in migration in sub-Saharan Africa, there remain significant knowledge gaps:

  - International remittances appear to be much smaller in Africa than in any other world region, representing just 10 per cent of external finance in 2001, compared to 63 per cent in South Asia, and 56 per cent in the Middle East and North Africa. However, this is partly because almost two thirds of sub-Saharan African countries simply do not report any data on remittances, suggesting that investment in monitoring systems would be of some value.

  - Data on the mobility of professionals in Africa remains poor, and might be best collected through cooperation with institutions in destination rather than sending countries. The complex relationships between international migration, training and labour market change also remain relatively underexplored.

- There is scope for the development of more effective regional policies on forced migration, which pay attention to the problems of long-term protracted refugee crises, the related economic, security and protection issues and the lack of solutions for many populations. The link to livelihoods is important here too, with a relative dearth of knowledge about effective livelihood strategies that are open to displaced populations.

- In thinking about policy on migration in sub-Saharan Africa, it is important to consider both migration policies per se, e.g. immigration control, facilitation of temporary and regional mobility, policies on refugees and trafficking, and also sectoral policies where migration is a relevant issue. The development of health and education strategies can be made more effective by taking into account the likely consequences of internal and international migration on resource allocation decisions, whilst policies to support poor people's livelihoods need to recognise the significance of migration as a livelihood strategy.

1.3 Data Issues

There are conflicting accounts of the volume of migration in contemporary Africa, reflecting the paucity of data sources and their often poor quality. According to the African Union, of the 190 million international migrants in the world, one third are estimated to be Africans.[1] In contrast, the ILO estimates that 20 million African men and women are migrant workers[2], IOM figures suggest that out of 175 million migrants worldwide, just 16.2 million are in Africa.[3] Zlotnik highlights only Côte d'Ivoire and South Africa as key countries of immigration on the continent.[4] Elsewhere, the size of foreign populations is either very small, or, in the absence of statistical systems to monitor flows, numbers are largely unknown. These figures do not include the large amount of undocumented cross-border migration within Africa, nor the extent of migration within countries.[5]

Table 1: Migrants as a proportion of the population	
Region	**% migrants**
Caribbean	2.9
Sub-Saharan Africa	2.8
Latin America	1.7
Asia	1.4
Source: UN	

One area in which Africa has long been prominent is in the production of refugees, where it accounts for a third or more of global totals. However, the numbers have been in steady decline since a peak of 6.8 million in 1995. The number has since fallen to 4.6 million at the start of 2003, largely as a result of significant repatriation to Rwanda from 1996. The main refugee-producing countries in Africa are now Burundi, Sudan, Somalia, Angola, Eritrea, Sierra Leone and Liberia, although significant repatriations have occurred to all of these, with the exception of Sudan.[6] There is also growing awareness of the extent of internal displacement in Africa, with an estimated 13 million IDPs dwarfing the number of refugees, and representing over half of the global total of IDPs.[7] These include an estimated 3 million in Sudan and 1.2 million in Uganda. Although there were some repatriations in 2003, new IDPs were created in the Democratic Republic of Congo (DRC), Uganda, Sudan, Liberia, and in the Central African Republic.

There is substantial and growing migration from key African countries to Europe and North America.[8] Data presented in Appendix 1 shows that from Africa as a whole, over 110,000 people left each year to go to Europe or the US between 1995-2001, with the number rising from 93,000 in 1995 to nearly 140,000 in 2001. Countries with higher than average annual rates of migration proportional to their population size were Somalia and Eritrea in East Africa; Ghana, Senegal, Cape Verde, Liberia, Sierra Leone, Mali, Gambia and Guinea-Bissau in West Africa; and South Africa, Namibia, Mauritius, the Seychelles and Comoros in Southern Africa.

Table 2: African-born residents in the US, 2000	
Country of birth	**Number**
Nigeria	134,940
Ethiopia	69,531
Ghana	65,572
South Africa	63,558
Sierra Leone	20,831
Source: US Census, 2000, cited at http://www.migrationinformation.org/Usfocus/print. cfm?ID=147	

In terms of absolute numbers, the key countries of long-distance emigration were Nigeria, South Africa, Ghana, Somalia, Ethiopia and Senegal. Of these, migration from South Africa, Somalia and Senegal is orientated primarily to Europe, Ethiopian emigration is orientated primarily to the US, and Nigerian and Ghanaian emigration is split evenly between the two.

There is rather less available data on flows of migrants within African countries, though evidence from micro-level studies suggests that this form of mobility is very substantial across most African countries. Relevant data may be available from censuses, although recent censuses in some countries such as Nigeria, Tanzania and Malawi do not include information on internal migration. Thirteen African countries have not held a census within the last ten years; many others have held them so recently that preliminary results are not yet available (Appendix 2).

Special surveys that include figures on internal migration are available in some countries. Living Standards Measurement Surveys (LSMS) in Ghana, South Africa, Tanzania and Côte d'Ivoire provide fairly reliable measures of household livelihoods as well as basic migration data.[9]

It is not possible on the basis of currently available data to generalise much about the demographic and socio-economic characteristics of internal and inter-regional migration within Africa, apart from noting that it involves men, women and children.[10] There is some evidence from countries such as Nigeria, Mali and Tanzania that the number of young female migrants has increased.[11] Predominant flows appear to be from rural to urban areas, although rural-rural migration is also significant in many countries, with areas of significant cash-crop production often recruiting large numbers of farm labourers from neighbouring regions. Only eight African countries have more than half of their population in towns.[12]

There is increasing evidence of links between migration and HIV/AIDS, although this tends to focus more on high HIV prevalence amongst migrants, rather than investigation of how the contraction of HIV/AIDS affects migration patterns and the value of migration as a livelihood strategy. Meanwhile, patterns of internal migration appear to have been affected by economic crisis and structural adjustment, with some arguing that a long trend of urbanisation across the continent has been stopped or even reversed.[13] However, much of the evidence for both urbanisation and counter-urbanisation remains anecdotal.

In contrast, slightly more confidence can be given to observations that African migration to Europe and North America is dominated by flows of more educated and, by implication, less poor individuals (see Table 3). This evidence is provided by the US Census and the SOPEMI reporting system of migration statistics for OECD countries. Based on 1990 census figures, it has been calculated that 95,000 out of 128,000 African migrants in the US at that time had a tertiary education, whilst migration of those with primary education or below was 'virtually zero'.[14]

Nonetheless, in most African countries, it appears that only a relatively small proportion of tertiary-educated individuals (and few others) had migrated to the US. The figure was over 5 per cent for Mozambique, Mauritius, Zambia and Zimbabwe, over 10 per cent for Kenya, Uganda and Ghana, around 25 per cent for Sierra Leone and a massive 60 per cent for Gambia.[15] When migration to other OECD countries is added, it was estimated that over a quarter of Ghanaians with tertiary education had left Ghana, whilst the figure for South Africa was around 8 per cent.

Table 3: Educational attainment of African-born population in US, 2000		
Country of birth	Proportion with 4 years schooling or less	Proportion with over 4 years tertiary education
Nigeria	7%	47%
Tanzania	4%	46%
Cameroon	6%	45%
Uganda	3%	45%
South Africa	8%	44%
Zimbabwe	6%	39%
Kenya	10%	36%
Sudan	15%	28%
Africa, ns/nec	8%	28%
Ghana	7%	26%
Senegal	9%	25%
Liberia	8%	25%
Ethiopia	8%	23%
Sierra Leone	9%	23%
Eritrea	10%	18%
Somalia	24%	9%
Africa total[1]	8%	33%
Source: calculated from 5% sample of US census		
Notes: 1. Figure for all residents born in Africa		

1.4 Migration Policy

Across sub-Saharan Africa as a whole, the position of governments towards migration generally remains either neutral or hostile. In a review by UNDESA, seven countries – Kenya, Gabon, Côte d'Ivoire, Botswana, Namibia, Djibouti, and Gambia – were reported as indicating in 2000 that levels of immigration were too high, whilst a further eleven reported that they had in place policies to reduce immigration.[16] Meanwhile, four – Gabon, Sudan, Burkina Faso, and Guinea-Bissau – reported that emigration was too high, and that their policy was to reduce emigration. In its most recent review of the status of poverty in Africa, the African Development Bank refers to rural-urban migration as a source of urban poverty. A recent position paper of the ILO on Working out of Poverty fails to mention migration as a relevant component of poverty or poverty reduction. In the UNDESA survey, only one country – Cape Verde

– considered that its level of emigration was too low, and even then, there was no explicit government policy to promote it.

One area in which concern is expressed about migration is the question of 'brain drain' of African professionals. This is said to hit the sectors of health, education and technological development particularly severely.[17] As African professionals leave the continent, an estimated US$4 billion is spent each year, mostly through overseas aid programmes, on hiring some 100,000 skilled expatriates to replace them.[18]

Box 1: Migration in the PRSPs

A review of PRSPs across Africa shows considerable ambivalence about migration. It is often simply not recognised as an issue, or not addressed. So, for example, in a total of seven sub-Saharan African PRSPs, migration is not mentioned at all, whilst in a further ten other countries, it is mentioned, but the anti-poverty strategies outlined in the document fail to then refer to it as an issue. In Burundi, the DRC and Sierra Leone, forced migration is considered, but other forms of migration are not.

Overwhelmingly, where economic migration is mentioned, it is seen as negative. For example, migration is seen as contributing to population growth (Gambia), placing pressure on urban areas (Gambia, Guinea, Mauritania), breaking down traditional family structures (Kenya, Malawi), promoting the spread of crime (Côte d'Ivoire, Malawi, Sierra Leone) and diseases such as HIV/AIDS (Burkina Faso, Niger, Sierra Leone), stimulating land degradation (Ethiopia) and reinforcing rural poverty (Côte d'Ivoire, Gambia, Malawi, Niger, Sierra Leone). Only Cape Verde and Senegal mention emigration as a positive factor, with the Cape Verde PRSP noting that restrictive measures in host countries have cut remittances, whilst the Niger and Rwanda PRSPs note that internal migration can boost household incomes of the poor.

Where policy responses to migration are mentioned, these are primarily geared to reducing or preventing migration, mainly through promoting rural development. However, some exceptions exist. For example, both Cape Verde and Senegal propose a strategy to promote remittances and engage emigrants in national development, whilst Mauritania suggests creating viable jobs in urban areas rather than trying to prevent rural-urban migration.

Source: Review of PRSPs, March 2004. See Appendix 3.

A number of policy responses have been put forward to address the 'brain drain'. At one level, intergovernmental initiatives, including through the African Union, have sought to improve the quality of tertiary education in Africa, and the circulation of students and professionals within Africa, to remove the necessity for Africans to go abroad for university training.[19] The African Virtual University, established by the World Bank in 1997, also operates in 17 African countries and has so far educated more than 24,000 students.

Where training does take place abroad, there are various mechanisms that might be put in place to encourage individuals to return. One positive example is provided by analysis of return amongst participants in AIDS Training and Research Programs funded by the Fogarty International Center, National Institutes of Health in the US, where nearly 80 per cent of African trainees returned, whether on masters, doctoral or post-doctoral training. The strategies used in this case included the building of health infrastructure in the trainee's home country, provision of re-entry research support and the use of short-stay visas and repayment agreements to discourage non-return.[20]

Another response at continent-wide level has been the development of links with Africans abroad, either to encourage them to return, or to utilise their skills, knowledge or financial capital in the promotion of African development. Online databases, which provide an opportunity for Africans abroad to advertise their skills, or for African companies or government bodies to advertise vacancies, have been advocated or established by organisations such as 'Africa's Brain Gain' (ABG)[21], Africa Recruit[22] and the Economic Commission for Africa.[23] There are also initiatives focused on specific sectors such as health[24] and law[25], as well as databases of diaspora members maintained by particular countries, including South Africa, Nigeria, Benin, and Burkina Faso.

The International Organisation for Migration has also established a 'Migration for Development in Africa' (MIDA) programme, which aims to build partnerships between host countries and countries of origin of migrants, and encourage the return of African professionals on temporary assignments.[26] In addition, some countries, such as Ghana, Senegal, Rwanda and Ethiopia, have organised meetings and conferences for members of the diaspora, whilst the Conference on Security, Stability, Development and Cooperation in Africa (CSSDCA) of the African Union organised the first 'AU-Western Hemisphere Diaspora Forum' in Washington DC in December 2002.[27]

At a continent-wide level, the African Union has established a 'strategic framework for a policy on migration', and a specific programme on migration within its Social Affairs Directorate. The programme's goals include addressing the causes of internal and international migration and the 'challenges posed by migration', but it also seeks cooperation between countries to 'make effective use of the opportunity presented by the phenomenon', and seeks to assist AU member states to work towards the free movement of people.[28] At the moment, this programme appears to exist on paper only; in contrast, the strategic framework was pushed forward at an experts meeting in Addis Ababa in March 2004.

Concern with the effects of migration has also filtered through into policymaking in specific sectors. The New Partnership for African Development (NEPAD) has not yet developed an overall policy or initiative on migration, but its strategy for the health sector does include proposed measures to mitigate the loss of health sector personnel, including the promotion of guidelines on ethical recruitment practices, and measures to improve conditions of service and work environments.[29] Attention also certainly needs to be paid to the factors creating shortages of doctors and nurses in recruiting countries, although this is clearly much more difficult for NEPAD or the AU to influence.

It is worth noting here that the impact of migration on health outcomes for poor people is felt not only through migration of health personnel to northern countries, but also through regional migration flows (e.g. to South Africa, Namibia and elsewhere), rural-urban migration within countries, and through 'migration' from the public to the private sector.[30] In this context, measures to promote improved telecommunications or the supply of drugs to rural clinics may have an impact in reducing movement of health personnel out of clinics serving the poorest, but expansion of training in the health sector in general – both in Africa and in the 'north' – also clearly needs to be part of the solution.

The migration of health personnel in Africa has also received the attention of the World Health Organisation, which conducted a study of over 2,000 health professionals across Ghana, Uganda, Cameroon, Zimbabwe, South Africa and Senegal in 2002.[31] This study found that availability of training, standard of living and working conditions were all significant factors encouraging health personnel to emigrate, and that their loss is having a significant impact in terms of increasing workload. This decreases motivation and quality of service provided by those who remain, who are often less skilled and unqualified to carry out specialised tasks.

There is also concern in some quarters that rich nations should pay some sort of compensation for medical personnel recruited out of Africa, given the structure of African health sector training in which the bulk of this training is publicly funded and provided. However, the Joint Learning Initiative on Human Resources for Health (HRH), funded by the Rockefeller Foundation, has stressed that whilst health systems are suffering attrition from international migration and internal displacement, they also face significant challenges from deteriorating conditions of employment, reduced effectiveness of delivery systems, an increase in disease burdens and a lack of financing for the sector from African governments.

A recent study of the movement of doctors and nurses from Ghana, Zimbabwe and South Africa to the UK critiques emerging WHO policy in this area.[32] It stresses that data are poor and might be better collected in destination countries. It also suggests that migration of medical personnel from Africa to the UK at least may be declining, whilst movement of nurses has recently increased dramatically.

In contrast to this attention to the brain drain, there appears to be rather less interest amongst African governments in migration as a livelihood strategy, or in the welfare of migrants, despite the fact that these relate more clearly to the poor and to pro-poor policy. Rather, traditional countries of immigration such as South Africa, Côte d'Ivoire and Gabon have become more intolerant of migrant workers. Regional blocks such as ECOWAS and SADC have generally failed to prioritise freedom of movement. Where attention has been paid to HIV/AIDS, this has tended to stigmatise migrants as potentially spreading the epidemic.[33] There has also been little attention to date to policies on currency exchange or the improvement and extension of banking systems in a way that would facilitate the flow of remittances.

In the field of forced migration in particular, there has been a tightening of policies towards refugees in a number of countries, reflecting growing global antipathy towards forced migrants.[34] States have cited the economic burdens involved, declining support from international donors, and the potential security threats (e.g. camps being used as rebel bases, local insecurity and cross-border attacks). In addition to some cases of expulsion of refugees, a major consequence appears to have been the increased use of camps with severe restrictions on movement, even though these have often failed to guarantee security and limit refugees' ability to contribute to their own livelihoods and the local economy.

Nonetheless, 11 African countries are signatories to the Migrant Workers Convention – more than in most other world regions.[35] The ILO has designed and launched an 'African Labour Migration Policy Initiative' which seeks to enhance the knowledge base on labour migration and build capacity of labour ministries and others to deal with labour migration.[36] IOM has conducted some preliminary work to identify and promote networking between initiatives to combat HIV/AIDS amongst migrant and mobile populations.[37] Some sectoral organisations have also promoted mobility: e.g. the Association of African Universities has called on African governments to bring in legislation to promote the mobility of academic staff and students.

Many African governments and international organisations pay most attention to the movement of skilled professionals to the US and Europe, and measures that might be taken to limit this flow, or encourage their return or engagement with development initiatives in their home countries. This is reflected in the regional and country sections that follow. However, although such linkages may be relevant to pro-poor policy, it is important to bear in mind that they may not; e.g. the private capital transfers of such migrants may not filter down to sectors of the economy where the poor are found, whilst the return of professionals may have little impact on services targeted at the poor.

In contrast, it is important not to ignore large-scale migration by the poor in search of livelihood, even if this has, to date, received less attention from governments and policymakers. A review of Africa-wide issues based on field studies in Mali, Nigeria and Tanzania notes that occupational diversification in rural areas is often inextricably linked to mobility, whilst 'migration has been a key factor in shaping Africa's settlement patterns and households' livelihoods'.[39] This study found that a staggering 50-80 per cent of rural households had at least one migrant member, across all wealth categories, and with increasing involvement of women as independent migrants (see Box 2).

Box 2: Migration and Poverty: trends in the 1990s

In work by IIED, strong linkages maintained between (rural) source and (urban) destination areas for migrants in Africa were found to:

• promote significant flows of remittances,
• encourage community level initiatives for the construction of public facilities and infrastructure,
• help link rural producers to urban markets.

However, the study also found that remittances had declined over a 15-year period, largely as a result of employment insecurity in destination areas, even though at the same time rural households had become more dependent on these remittances. In turn, public policy had failed to recognise the spatial and occupational complexity of rural and urban livelihoods.

Source: Tacoli (2002); see endnote 11.

The potential for remittances to contribute to national development priorities, including the reduction of poverty, is clearly a priority for policymakers across the continent. However, it is worth noting – in contrast to comments globally that remittances constitute a 'stable source of external development finance' – that remittances in Africa appear highly volatile, at least in terms of official IMF figures.[40] The standard deviation from annual average remittance figures between 1980-99 was over 50 per cent in the cases of Cameroon, Cape Verde, Niger and Togo, and over 100 per cent in Botswana, Lesotho and Nigeria. In Burkina Faso, official remittances dropped from $187 million in 1988 to just $67 million in 1999, a decrease of two thirds, which coincided with a sharp drop in GDP growth rates.[41]

If official figures are to be believed, international remittances are much smaller in Africa than in any other world region, representing just 10 per cent of external finance in 2001, compared to 63 per cent in South Asia, and 56 per cent in the Middle East and North Africa.[42] In part, this is because almost two thirds of sub-Saharan African countries simply do not report any data on remittances, suggesting that investment in monitoring systems would be of some value.[43]

There is also scope for the development of more coordinated regional policies on forced migration, given the prominence of forced migration across the continent. Although most African countries are signatories to the 1969 OAU Convention[44], and many in practice recognise refugees en masse, or devolve responsibility to UNHCR for the processing of refugee claims, there have been calls for a change of approach from some quarters (e.g. the mixed assistance and protection mandate of UNHCR has been called into question).[45] Attention also needs to be paid to the problems of long-term protracted refugee crises, the related economic, security and protection issues and the lack of solutions up to now. The link to livelihoods is important here too, since a livelihoods approach to forced migrants may be just as valid as to poor people in general.

The sections below explore these issues in more depth in relation to three major regions of sub-Saharan Africa, and specifically in relation to Nigeria, Ghana, Sierra Leone and Liberia in West Africa; Kenya, Tanzania, Uganda and Rwanda in East Africa; and South Africa. Each section considers the impact of migration on the poor, and policy responses that have sought to curtail, manage or mobilise the opportunities presented by migration. Key policy themes across each of these regions and countries include a clear concern with the loss of skilled professionals and with the trafficking of women and children, but examples are also reported where migration has had potentially positive outcomes for the poor, and how these positive outcomes might be maximised.

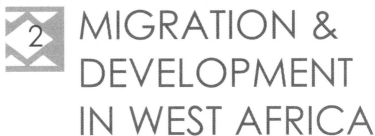 MIGRATION & DEVELOPMENT IN WEST AFRICA

2.1 Overview

- West Africa has a long history of population mobility, both regionally and internationally. Linked with factors as diverse as long-distance trade; the search for pasture; urbanisation and the growth of administrative centres; the demands of mining, industrial production and plantation agriculture; armed conflict; land degradation; drought and rural poverty, migration has played a major part in shaping settlement patterns. It is estimated that one third of West Africans live outside their village of birth. Contemporary West African migrants are found in significant numbers around the world.

- Most West African countries were net losers of population from 1995-2000. In particular, countries such as Ghana and Nigeria have undergone a 'reverse migration transition', moving from being net immigration to net emigration countries.

- Monetary transfers made by migrants in the region are substantial, and have come to constitute a major source of income for many households in the context of economic decline, retrenchment of public services and adverse environmental conditions. Migrants also represent an important source of energy, ideas and improved agricultural management techniques in many rural areas.

- Both internal and international flows in West Africa appear to have diversified in recent years, with more regions and countries producing migrants, and these migrants moving to a range of new destinations.

Movement to Europe and North America is higher than in other parts of the continent, and is dominated by young men and women.

- There is emerging concern, but also controversy, over the level of trafficking in the region, including of children. There is also continuing concern about forced migration both regionally and internally, although conflict resolution efforts in Sierra Leone and Liberia have already produced some substantial return movements.

- A sizeable amount of West African migration is orientated to the UK, with significant groups from Nigeria, Ghana and Sierra Leone, as well as other countries in the region. These groups are also often organised into hometown, ethnic, alumni and other organisations, making this a fertile area for engagement with diaspora groups. Such engagement could seek to learn from the experience of these groups, and facilitate their investment in pro-poor policy initiatives and the promotion of conflict resolution and good governance across the region.

- There is technically freedom of movement within the ECOWAS zone, but migrant workers' rights are not always respected. The Dakar Declaration, a regional process initiated by IOM in 2000 and signed by most West African countries, serves as a plan of action to promote the protection of migrants and to strengthen their role in development. Attention could also be paid to promoting an ECOWAS initiative to introduce regional passports, although regional action to address conflict and mass displacement may be a more urgent priority.

- Unlike much of sub-Saharan Africa, PRSPs in some West African countries do acknowledge the importance of migration for poor people's livelihoods – notably those in Cape Verde, Mali and Niger.

- West African governments have recently sought to prioritise either the return of their diasporas, and/or the promotion of financial investments in the country by those living abroad. However, there may also be scope to facilitate the trading and business networks that some diaspora communities have developed abroad in a way that is of benefit to West African economies. One study of West Africans in New York shows how they have successfully marketed authentic 'African' products to the large African American community of the city. This suggests that there may be some scope for increased trade flows that could benefit the region.

- Trafficking in West Africa is seen by many agencies as 'pervasive and growing', leading to both child labour and sexual exploitation of women. However, problems with definitions of trafficking, and especially 'traffickers' are highlighted by a recent study of the causes, context and consequences of youth migration from central Mali. The types of hardship experienced by migrant children may be similar whether or not they cross international borders. The use of an intermediary may also be obligatory for any child wishing to migrate, yet it is often impossible to determine whether these intermediaries have an intention to exploit. Often NGO and government initiatives to return trafficked children to their villages have been met with unhappiness from children, incredulity from parents, and teasing and humiliation from the children's peer group.

- A number of knowledge gaps remain in relation to migration within and from West Africa:

  - Some countries, such as Ghana, have relatively good population and migration statistics, but the same is not true for countries such as Sierra Leone and Liberia that are emerging from periods of armed conflict, and in which social research capacity has been severely weakened.

  - In Nigeria, there is also a major dearth of data on migration, reflecting the poor quality of social and demographic statistics more generally. However, with a new census planned for this year, there is a prospect of improved data becoming available, and resources could be allocated to ensure it is properly analysed.

  - A particularly poorly understood area is that of the migration of children, whose movement is often denied or characterised as forced, but which in reality may be somewhat more complex. Attention could usefully be focused on seeking to understand these flows, as well as prioritising the reduction of harm and exploitation rather than the prevention of all child migration.

- Regional policy initiatives are starting to appear in West Africa that hold out the prospect of more effective policies on migration. The Sahel and West Africa Club of the OECD has recently published a study on West Africa in the context of globalisation, which includes attention to migration. It also organised a conference in 2003 on the Mano River Union region and Côte d'Ivoire, which explored the relationship between migration, displacement and conflict.

- Discussions on regional integration are also advancing, and this presents an opportunity to raise the issue of regional mobility, both of skilled professionals and unskilled workers. However, fears about migration, including within countries, are real and need to be addressed. For example, policies to promote improved tenure rights for poor people over land, forests and mineral resources remain divisive, at least in part since they can exacerbate tensions between migrants and 'indigenous' populations of particular areas.

2.2 Region-Wide Issues

West Africa has a long history of population mobility, both internally and externally. Côte d'Ivoire is one of the top ten countries of destination for migrants worldwide according to figures collated by the IOM, with some 3 million immigrants making up a quarter of its population. Migrants have also historically moved to Nigeria, Senegal, Ghana and the Gambia. Major countries of emigration are Burkina Faso, Niger and Mali. According to De Haan[46], around one third of West Africans live outside their district or village of birth, whilst 42 per cent of the total number of international migrants residing in Africa are located in West Africa.[47] Historically, labourers have moved to work in plantation agriculture, the mining industry, centres of oil and industrial production, and administrative centres. Trade, war and harsh physical environments have also led to highly mobile livelihoods across the region.[48]

Over a thirty-year period from 1960-90, it has been estimated that international migration alone involved 7.2 million people, excluding Nigeria, representing around 11 per cent of the median population of the region in that period.[49] More recent UNDESA figures suggest that most West African countries were net losers of population from 1995-2000, with the exception of Côte d'Ivoire, Gambia, Liberia and Togo (Table 4).

In the latter two countries, net immigration from 1995-2000 reflects return of nationals during this period, whilst the high migrant stocks shown in Table 4 for Burkina Faso, Liberia and Togo probably represent nationals of those countries who were born abroad and subsequently moved 'back' to their country of nationality, rather than immigration of nationals of other countries.

Despite long-established patterns of migration in the region, it is worth noting that there has been considerable volatility in West African migration patterns over recent years:

- First, expulsions of migrants from Ghana in 1969, Nigeria in 1983 and 1985, and violence against foreigners living in Côte d'Ivoire in the aftermath of the 2000 elections has led to significant return movements of West African migrants from neighbouring states, with some fundamental impacts on migration and settlement patterns.

Table 4: Selected development and migration indicators for West African countries

Country	Population (millions) 2000	GDP per capita (US$ PPP) 2000[1]	Human Development Index (HDI) 2000[2]	Migrant stock (%) 2000[3]	Average annual net migration rate (per 1000) 1995-2000
Benin	6.3	990	0.420	1.6	-3.2
Burkina Faso	11.5	976	0.325	9.7	-5.5
Cape Verde	0.4	4,863	0.715	2.4	-2.5
Côte d'Ivoire	16.0	1,630	0.428	14.6	0.8
Gambia	1.3	1,649	0.405	14.2	9.1
Ghana	19.3	1,964	0.548	3.2	-1.2
Guinea	8.2	1,982	0.414	9.1	-6.2
Guinea-Bissau	1.2	755	0.349	1.6	-2.9
Liberia	2.9	..	..	5.5	36.5
Mali	11.4	797	0.386	0.4	-4.7
Mauritania	2.7	1,677	0.438	2.3	3.4
Niger	10.8	746	0.277	1.1	-0.1
Nigeria	113.9	896	0.462	0.7	-0.2
Senegal	9.4	1,510	0.431	3.0	-1.1
Sierra Leone	4.4	490	0.275	1.1	-7.8
Togo	4.5	1,442	0.493	4.0	6.1

Source: Figures compiled by Jørgen Carling from UNDP and UN Population Division.

Notes: 1. Purchasing Power Parity (PPP) is an adjustment of the Gross Domestic Product to account for price differences across countries and allow comparison of real incomes.

2. The Human Development Index is calculated on the basis of statistics on life expectancy at birth, adult literacy rate, gross educational enrolment ratio and GDP per capita (PPP, $US).

3. Refers to the percentage of the population born outside the country, except figures for Guinea, Mali, Mauritania, Nigeria and Sierra Leone, which refer to percentage of the population with foreign citizenship.

- Second, conflicts notably in Liberia and Sierra Leone have made West Africa host to one of the continent's larger refugee populations, although significant returns have now occurred both to these countries, and to some other countries affected by civil strife, including Togo, Mali and Guinea-Bissau.

- Third, whilst urbanisation accelerated in the period 1960-80, it is thought to have slowed considerably since then, if Nigeria is excluded from the analysis.[50] Moreover, although urbanisation has occurred, rural population densities across the region have nonetheless continued to rise.

Movement to Europe and North America also appears to have been higher in West Africa than in other parts of the continent. Figures from the 2000 US census show that West Africans made up more than half of those born in sub-Saharan Africa, with most entering the country since 1990. Data from EUROSTAT and other sources for the period 1985-93 suggests that 415,000 West Africans already lived in Europe at that time, around a third (128,000) in France, followed by the UK (82,000), Germany (74,000) and Italy (63,000).[51]

Migration routes to Europe have traditionally followed old colonial linkages, with the bulk of West Africans in France coming from Francophone countries, and those in the UK coming from Nigeria, Ghana, Gambia and Sierra Leone. However, diversification of flows was already evident in 1990 both to other European destinations (see Box 3), and from a wider range of West African countries of origin (e.g. Benin, Burkina Faso, Guinea). EUROSTAT data suggests around 60 per cent of West Africans in Europe are aged 20-39. They also show migration to Europe to have been on a distinct upward trajectory in the last decade, although the absence of flow data for some countries makes time series comparisons problematic.

Box 3: Diversification in international flows from West Africa

In the last year for which official data on new arrivals was available in all EU countries, Italy had become the most important destination for West Africans who moved legally, with just under 10,000 entrants. Of these, roughly one third came from Senegal, and a further 20 per cent each from Nigeria and Ghana. The next largest European destination was Portugal, with just over 5,000 entrants, the vast majority from Cape Verde and Guinea-Bissau, followed by the UK and France. Germany, which had admitted more than 10,000 West Africans in 1996, with two thirds coming from Nigeria and the Democratic Republic of Congo alone, fell to just 1,440 entrants in 1999, though rose to over 5,000 in 2001, whilst France also saw a dramatic decline from over 13,000 entrants in 1998 to just under 4,000 in 1999. In contrast, the numbers going legally to the UK, Spain and Portugal rose considerably at the end of the 1990s.

Source: Data from Eurostat

Table 5: Senegalese migrants worldwide			
Destination	**Registered**	**Non-registered**	**Total**
Côte d'Ivoire	50,000	100,000	150,000
France	45,000	60,000	105,000
Gambia			100,000
Italy			60,000
Mauritania	12,000	45,000	57,000
Egypt	2,000	30,000	32,000
North America	3,200	15,000	18,200
Iberian peninsula			Over 15,000
Gabon			15,000
Germany	1,500	5,000	Over 6,500
Total	113,700	255,000	Over 558,700
Source: Diatta and Mbow, 1999, see endnote 53.			

Yet figures for legal migration clearly only tell a part of the story. Legal entry to the US from Africa has remained fairly level over the last decade, but substantial communities of West Africans have built up, including people entering and overstaying on tourist or student visas who are not counted by official immigration statistics. It has been estimated that there are as many as 35,000 to 40,000 Senegalese in the New York area alone, many of whom are believed to have entered or remained in the US illegally.[52] Data on the Senegalese diaspora have been compiled by Diatta and Mbow, showing over half a million Senegalese living outside Senegal, at least half of whom are not officially registered in their country of destination (Table 5).[53]

A number of key themes emerge in relation to migration in West Africa. These include:

- Substantial levels of mobility, internally, regionally and internationally, with long historical roots, and impacting significantly on the poor. This includes substantial rural-rural as well as rural-urban flows.

- A diversification of migration flows in recent years (see Box 3), with countries such as Ghana, Nigeria, and more recently Côte d'Ivoire undergoing a 'reverse migration transition', moving from being countries of immigration to countries of emigration.

- Emerging concern, but also controversy, over the level and nature of 'trafficking' within the region (see Boxes 4 and 6).

- A history of expulsions of migrant workers in some countries, and a continuing high degree of political sensitivity over migration (see Box 5).

- Attempts by governments in a number of countries to reach out to diaspora groups living in Europe and North America (see Box 7).

- Continuing concern about forced migration both regionally and internally, although conflict resolution efforts in e.g. Sierra Leone, Liberia, and Mali have already produced substantial return movements.

In the following sections, these themes are merged both in relation to their impact on the poor, and in terms of long-distance international migration that tends to be the preserve of more educated, less-poor individuals. Trends in Francophone West Africa and the region as a whole are briefly reviewed, before sections that deal with Nigeria, Ghana, and Sierra Leone and Liberia in more detail.

Box 4: Alternative views on trafficking

Problems with definitions of trafficking, and especially 'traffickers' are highlighted by a recent study of the causes, context and consequences of youth migration from central Mali. This study suggests that types of hardship experienced by migrant children were similar whether or not they had crossed international borders, or could be considered to have been trafficked, whilst many revealed positive migration experiences. It also shows how in a sample of over 100 Malian children working in Abidjan and the cocoa, coffee, cotton, yam and cashew plantations of Côte d'Ivoire, all of whom had been identified as victims of trafficking, only four turned out to have actually been handled by a trafficker.

The study highlights how the focus on 'traffickers' is problematic in the West African context, where use of an intermediary is almost obligatory for any child wishing to migrate, yet it is often impossible to determine whether these intermediaries have an intention to exploit. It also notes that NGO and government initiatives to return trafficked children to their villages have been met with unhappiness from children, incredulity from parents, and teasing and humiliation from the children's peer group.

Source: Castle and Diarra (2003); see endnote 70.

2.3 Importance of Migration to the Poor

Across West Africa, migration represents a significant livelihood strategy for poor people. As noted above, this is a factor that is recognised in Poverty Reduction Strategy Papers (PRSPs) in Cape Verde, Senegal and Niger, but it is certainly not restricted to these countries (e.g. until the recent civil war in Côte d'Ivoire, around a quarter of Burkina Faso's GDP came from remittances from that country).[54] Evidence from a recent study of remittance behaviour by over 800 immigrant household heads in Abidjan suggests that monetary transfers to family members both outside the country, and those living in other parts of Côte d'Ivoire, remained substantial even during the civil war, and mainly take the form of cash transfers to support basic household expenditure.[55]

In Senegal, a country widely acknowledged to have benefited from migration, it is estimated that nearly $1 million is transferred to the Bank de l'Habitat du Senegal from Libreville every month[56], whilst somewhere between 30 and 80 per cent of household budgets in Senegal are said to be comprised of remittances.[57] These are transfers that affect all social classes. Roy Stacy, Program Director of the Famine Early Working System (FEWS) Network, noted in evidence to a recent congressional caucus that deregulation, liberalisation of trade and freer movement of labour in West Africa as part of the Sahel Development Plan had led to a 'spatial redistribution of people with approximately 8.0 million Sahelians dispersing into other parts of West Africa. Many of these migrants are now an important source of capital, ideas and improved agriculture management techniques which flow back into the Sahel as a result of the livelihoods diversification that has occurred with the labour mobility'.[58] In contrast, restriction of mobility has been seen as a cause of land degradation as it leads to conversion of grazing to cropland.

Internal migration, between and within urban and rural areas, continues to account for most migratory movements in West Africa. But in some countries, such as Burkina Faso, international migration outweighs internal migration.[59] Many individuals as well as entire families move out of hostile areas characterised by drought and low agricultural productivity in search of richer lands to farm or a remunerated job in town. Many of these movements are temporary or seasonal. They help the rural poor in supplementing farm earnings during the off-season, while keeping rights over their land.[60] Destinations have become more diversified and migrant itineraries more complex partly due to changes in wage-labour employment opportunities.

Rural to urban migration has contributed to the growth of cities, but a series of national surveys conducted simultaneously in eight West African countries in the 1990s shows that urban growth rates have declined in the region compared to the 1970s.[61] These surveys also reveal the prominent role played by female migration in contemporary urbanisation processes.

In turn, rural-rural flows, often (but not always) over shorter distances and for a few months rather than years, may often be the most important to the poor and in times of economic hardship. A study in the Sahel during the drought years of the mid-1980s found that as the drought took hold, long-distance migration actually declined, possibly because people could not afford the up-front investment involved in migration, but that temporary circulation over shorter distances increased considerably.[62] Such 'distress' migration may be a key factor in keeping poor households from starvation. More generally there is a relative paucity of studies focusing on rural to rural seasonal flows, although some recent studies are noted in the section on Ghana below.

Whilst migration has a number of positive benefits, problematic aspects of migration are noted in the literature that may specifically impact the poorest. The FAO has argued that mobility of members of farming households is partly responsible for seasonal labour shortages and an ageing of on-farm populations, with a negative effect on agricultural productivity.[63] In addition, trafficking in West Africa (see Box 4) is seen by many agencies as 'pervasive and growing', falling into two main types:

- trafficking of children mainly for domestic and agricultural work both across and within national borders; and

- trafficking in women and children for sexual exploitation, mainly to outside the region.[64]

Although figures are often provided on the extent of these two phenomena, they are often unreliable.

2.4 Migration Policies in West Africa

Within the Economic Community of West African States (ECOWAS) there is technically freedom of movement, and significant numbers of West African nationals are living in neighbouring countries. Yet such movement is not always officially recognised, or indeed tolerated. The history of expulsions of foreign workers is reflected in increasingly restrictive attitudes in key countries of immigration such as Côte d'Ivoire and Gabon, as well as widespread harassment and denial of rights. One response has been proposals at a regional level to introduce ECOWAS passports, which would provide an opportunity for holders to gain residence, employment and other rights in other ECOWAS countries, but such passports probably remain some way off.[65]

There are several areas in which policies and initiatives have been developed. First, regional action to address conflict and mass displacement has included ECOMOG interventions in conflicts in Liberia and Sierra Leone, and regional efforts to bring a resolution to the conflict in Côte d'Ivoire. In addition, a number of more recent initiatives to end conflict and promote development across the area of the Mano River Region and in neighbouring Côte d'Ivoire were discussed at a recent conference of the Sahel and West Africa Club of the OECD, recognising the extent to which national borders in the region cut across ethnic divisions and traditional migration routes.[66]

Second, there has been considerable regional attention to the issue of trafficking. ECOWAS members adopted a Political Declaration and Action Plan against trafficking in human beings in the West African region in December 2001, which called, amongst other things, for the creation of special anti-trafficking police units and a regional task force to deal with the issue.[67]

A review of national policies by UNICEF in 2002 has highlighted varied responses and perceptions, ranging from Mali, which was the first country in the region to adopt a 'National Emergency Plan to Fight against Child Trafficking', to Benin, which has so far taken no action, and Burkina Faso, where a plan is still under discussion and policy interest is low.[68] Bilateral agreements on combating trafficking have been reached between Côte d'Ivoire and Mali and Burkina Faso, and between Benin and Nigeria and Togo.[69] However, such policies, based on the UN Protocol to Prevent, Suppress and Punish Trafficking in Persons, Especially Women and Children can be questioned (see Box 4).[70]

Third, across West Africa, there have been efforts by governments to reach out to diaspora communities in Europe and North America, largely with an eye to encouraging their return to, or investment in their country of origin. These are described in more detail in sections on individual countries below, but there are also some important initiatives from Francophone countries, including some that involve the private sector and/or civil society.

The 2003 World Migration Report relates how three Paris-based banks have offered special transfer schemes to Côte d'Ivoire, Mali and Senegal with much lower fees than money courier services. At the same time, the phenomenon of co-development or 'coopération decentralisée' in which development initiatives are funded by migrants through home town associations or local NGOs is widespread across the region. Such 'translocal' initiatives fund work on irrigation, drinking water, roads, health centres, schools, literacy programmes, and measures to combat environmental degradation, and sometimes include mechanisms to lever public funds, such as town twinning arrangements between municipalities in Europe and towns or villages in Africa.[71]

Policy initiatives have been developed in several areas, but various gaps remain at a regional level. First, although individual governments have sought to encourage return of their diasporas, there may also be scope to facilitate the trading and business networks that some diaspora communities have developed abroad (e.g. a study of West Africans in New York shows how they have successfully marketed authentic 'African' products to the large African American community of the city, in a way that suggests some scope for increased trade flows that could benefit the region).[72]

Second, there is in practice relatively little in the way of regional policy initiatives on migration and development. Some steps toward a more effective management of migration have been taken with the establishment of a regional consultative process. One of the outcomes of this process, which was initiated in 2000 by the IOM and the International Migration Policy Programme (IMP), is the Dakar Declaration signed by most West African countries and serving as a plan of action to promote the protection of migrants and to strengthen their role in development.[73]

Whereas this kind of process has the advantage of fostering an open dialogue among governments on migration issues, it has been criticised for being too informal and non-binding. There are also some bilateral agreements between West African countries, which could be expanded (e.g. Senegal signed a pro-tocol agreement with Gabon in 1987, which secured social security benefits for the children of Senegalese workers, whether or not they were living with these workers in Gabon).[74] Such bilateral agreements across important migra-tion 'dyads' (e.g. Burkina Faso-Côte d'Ivoire, Togo-Ghana) could be valuable in promoting migrant workers' rights and enhancing the potential benefits of intra-regional migration.

Third, whilst at a national level, it has been common for concern to be focused on limiting the 'brain drain' of nationals and (more recently) linking with migrant diasporas, there is considerable scope for enhanced cooperation across West Africa to create a more integrated labour market for professionals within the region, in order to provide clearer paths for career development and training at a regional level.

2.5 Nigeria

2.5.1 Introduction

Nigeria has been a major international migration destination in the past, although this flow was affected by civil strife in the 1970s, and was dramatically reversed with the expulsion of about a million Ghanaian and other foreign workers in 1983.[75] Since that time, migration in Nigeria has been characterised by emigration, as well as substantial amounts of internal migration. As elsewhere in the region, this has involved considerable rural-urban migration, including both permanent and temporary moves for work, education and to escape drought conditions in the northern Sahel areas in the early 1970s and again in the early 1980s.[76] A World Bank report in 1996 suggested that the pace of urbanisation is such that 60 per cent of the population will be urban by 2010.[77] A recent report by an NGO, 'Cities Alliance', suggested that the population of Abuja triples every year, in the fastest process of urbanization in West Africa.[78] In contrast, unlike many other countries of the region, there has been relatively little circular migration between rural areas, as Nigeria has a relatively underdeveloped plantation economy.

Box 5: Migration as a 'driver of change'

An overview of migration as a 'driver of change' in Nigeria has recently been completed for DFID Nigeria. The study's draft report generally paints a negative view of the impact of migration on the poor.

Highlighting rural-urban and forced migration as the key components of current flows, the report notes overcrowding in cities, with negative effects on public health, unemployment, and the threat of violence, as well as rising prices of staple foods as labour shortages appear in rural areas.

Going on to analyse the 'drivers of pro-poor change', the report identifies demographic growth and greater pressure on land, the increased 'manufacture' of ethnicity relating to land claims, deteriorating infrastructure, and discrimination against pastoralists as all stimulating additional migration that is negative in its consequences.

The paper also recognises the lack of both statistics and recent literature on internal migration in Nigeria, which it describes as 'tailing off' in the 1980s.

Source: Blench (2004); see endnote 92.

Aside from rural-urban migration, internal migration in recent years has been increasingly characterised by forced displacement by conflicts over crude oil mining and refining, communal conflicts, and conflicts associated with the democratisation process. One recent study has suggested the number of forced migrants in Nigeria is currently as high as 1.2 million, although none are 'of concern' to UNHCR.[79]

Nigerians are almost certainly the largest single national group amongst Africans living in Europe and North America, although as a proportion of Nigeria's vast population this type of movement is rather less significant than in many of Nigeria's neighbours.

2.5.2 Importance of Migration to the Poor

There are relatively few studies that consider directly the impact of migration on the poor in Nigeria. According to one study, rural-urban migration has led to rural depopulation and loss of agricultural production, as well as strains on urban areas.[80] Another notes how economic crisis and structural adjustment has dramatically reduced urban incomes, leading to declining remittances and weakening social ties, but without the urban-rural return migration that has occurred in some other regions of Africa.[81] The World Bank's Poverty Assessment for the country suggests that rural poverty is declining, and urban poverty increasing, largely due to rural-urban migration. The report suggests that there is a need 'to design growth policies which focus on (the urban poor), as well as measures to slow down the pace of migration'.[82]

However, other studies are more upbeat. A study by the International Institute for Environment and Development (IIED) in the south-east of the country found that investment of remittances in assets such as housing, land or livestock has been linked to intention to return, and has helped to fuel a construction boom that has stimulated local economic growth.[83] The migration of Fulani pastoralists to southwestern Nigeria is also said by one study to have produced positive economic results, e.g. stimulating the trade in cattle.[84]

One negative feature of migration in Nigeria appears to have been its impact on the status and/or well-being of women. A study of migration in Bendel state in the 1980s found that migrant women had not gained economically from movement to Benin City, but had suffered a loss of status within the household in comparison with non-migrant women.[85] There is also growing concern over a more direct attack on women's status and well-being in the form of trafficking of women and young girls to Europe, the Middle East and other parts of Africa.

Nigerian women are believed to be sent into commercial sex work in various European countries as well as Côte d'Ivoire and South Africa, whilst children are sent into domestic labour within Nigeria and in neighbouring countries. One recent press article stated that '10,000 Nigerian prostitutes were said to be in over 300 brothels in Germany, Spain and other parts of Europe and South America'.[86] Children from Togo, Benin, Ghana and Cameroon are also believed to be brought to Nigeria for forced labour.[87]

2.5.3 International Migration and the Brain Drain

Nearly 15,000 Nigerians migrated legally to Europe and North America every year from 1995-2001 (Appendix 1), whilst there are estimated to be some 200,000 to 300,000 first- and second-generation Nigerians living in the US[88], including perhaps as many as 21,000 Nigerian doctors.[89] A recent study based on 2000 census figures showed that of 109,000 Nigerian-born immigrants in the US aged 25 or over, some 90,000 were tertiary educated.[90] In Europe, it is estimated that there are some 45,000 Nigerians in the UK, 17,000 in Italy, and 15,000 in Germany, and although these migrants may be less well educated than those in the US, it remains likely that their level of education overall is high.[91] There is also significant movement to the Middle East, associated with the movement of pilgrims to Mecca.[92]

The exodus of Nigerian academics and students is said both to reflect and to have reinforced a decline in standards of university education in Nigeria.[93] High grade requirements and a limited number of places in Nigerian universities are also seen as encouraging attendance at college overseas, especially in the US.[94] As a result, there are now said to be more Nigerian academics in the US than in Nigeria, with many not assuming jobs in relevant fields but working instead as taxi drivers, factory workers, or in other unskilled or low-skilled occupations. However, it is not possible to estimate what proportion of educated Nigerians leave each year, as reliable figures on the number of university graduates are not available. Blench argues that the movement of Nigerians to the developed world is 'highly diverse', and 'certainly not the outflow of skilled labour it is sometimes portrayed as'.[95]

The international migration of highly skilled and other Nigerians to developed countries is not entirely negative. A study by the Federal Reserve Bank of Chicago has estimated that Nigerians in the US alone send $1.3 billion each year, or more than six times the annual flow of US aid to Nigeria. A small sample survey of just over 100 Nigerians in Chicago found average remittances of $6,000 per year, with 60 per cent of this going to basic household needs, and remittances higher where households in Nigeria are poorer, other factors being held constant.[96] Financial flows can also go in the opposite direction e.g. there appear to be substantial outflows of Nigerian oil wealth to Nigerians abroad.[97]

2.5.4 Migration Policies

The Nigerian government has put considerable effort into contacting Nigerian professionals abroad. President Obasanjo has met with Nigerian professionals living abroad to encourage their return, and has set up an 'Office of the Special Assistant to Mr. President on Diaspora Activities'.[98] The Senate has abolished a measure which meant that Nigerians abroad who had become citizens of other countries lost their Nigerian citizenship.[99] The Federal government has established a 'Diaspora Trust Fund', and has also discussed the establishment of a database of Nigerian professionals abroad.[100] This government activity complements an already-existing abundance of civil society initiatives, including numerous Nigerian hometowns and alumni associations, which represent professional interests as well as channelling remittances.[101]

The Nigerian government has put effort into enhanced law enforcement and better protection including a systematic repatriation network for trafficked children, although the United States Department of State argues that Nigeria still does not fully comply with minimum standards for the elimination of trafficking.[102] Several ministries sponsor information campaigns on children's rights and child labour; the Nigerian Immigration Service has created a Human Trafficking Unit; a comprehensive anti-trafficking law was passed in March 2003, whilst anti-trafficking police units were created in 11 states considered to be affected by trafficking. A Federal anti-trafficking unit is said to have been particularly active in Edo state, the primary source state for women trafficked to Italy.[103]

Despite these initiatives, there appears to be something of a lack of Nigerian government attention to migration. Measures to address rural-urban migration have been tried in the past, although apparently with little success in stemming such population movements. A policy on the dispersal of industries has not substantially changed the location of these industries, whilst minimum wage policy and low prices paid to farmers if anything reinforce the tendency for people to leave rural areas.[104] Internal displacement of Nigerians has been largely ignored by state and federal authorities.

Measures to curb rural-urban and other internal migrations remain popular in some quarters within Nigeria. A recent statement by the Presidential Advisor on Agriculture noted that 'Nigeria has the highest migration level in the world … with nearly 5 per cent per annum. It means that cities like Abuja, Lagos and Port Harcourt will become impossible to manage in the next 15 to 20 years', leading in turn to increased crime and other social problems.[105] Meanwhile, an opinion piece in the Abuja-based Daily Trust in 2002 called for sedentarisation of nomads, both to end clashes between nomads and pastoralists, and to allow better delivery of education and health services.

According to Blench, 'a failure to analyse or structure migration is having significant negative social and economic consequences' in Nigeria.[106] What is needed is improved data collection, a rational policy framework, as well as attention to discriminatory policies that have fuelled violence and conflict-induced migration. Certainly the absence of statistics or other robust data on either internal or international migration limits the ability of governments at federal, state or local level to take into account the impact of migration on pro-poor policy.

As noted above, there has also been little public policy orientated to meeting the needs of displaced Nigerians, with the bulk of assistance being provided by philanthropic individuals, families and social networks. In the Niger delta, oil companies have provided some relief assistance; but elsewhere, displaced people are often excluded from economic resources and opportunities as 'non-indigenes' in their place of asylum.[107]

2.6 Ghana

2.6.1 Overview

Like Nigeria, Ghana has a complex migration history, witnessing something of a migration 'turnaround' from being a country of immigration during the colonial era to being one of emigration in the 1970s and 1980s, as economic and political conditions worsened. EUROSTAT estimates that approximately 10 per cent of Ghana's population of 19 million currently lives abroad, principally in Nigeria, the US, Canada, Germany, Italy and the UK. Only recently, with the establishment of an apparently robust multi-party democratic system, and a more dynamic economy, has significant return to Ghana started to become feasible, and immigration from neighbouring countries has restarted.

> ## Box 6: Trafficking and child fostering
>
> Despite domestic and international concern about trafficking in Ghana, the movement of children cannot be viewed without reference to the practice of child fostering, which is widespread (as in many other countries in the region).
>
> Authors differ in their views of child fostering. One study of women from the South Volta region engaged in low-paid work in Accra found children being sent to relatives in rural areas ostensibly for education, but in practice ending up in highly abusive and exploitative situations. Another study found that child fostering was practiced by wealthy and poor alike, often leading to positive outcomes for both family and child.
>
> *Source: Population and Development Review 11 (1985).*

Ghana has also begun to host small numbers of refugees from neighbouring countries, with around 20,000 new arrivals from Liberia during 2002.[108] However, perhaps of most importance to the poor is the very large scale of internal migration within Ghana, estimated at well over 50 per cent of the population according to data compiled from the Ghana Living Standards Survey (GLSS).[109]

2.6.2 Importance of Migration to the Poor

Internal migration in Ghana is primarily from north to south, with in-migrants representing over 40 per cent of the population in the Greater Accra, Volta and Western regions. The role of migrant labour in the development of the cocoa and coffee industries in the 1960s and 1970s has been well-documented, with Eastern, Ashanti and Brong Ahafo regions receiving internal migration mainly from Northern, Upper East and Upper West regions.[110] There has also been substantial movement to mining areas, and rural-urban migration, especially to the major cities of Accra and Kumasi. The latter flow appears to have slowed, or possibly even reversed in the last decade.[111]

A classic study of migration from the Upper East region showed that migration at any particular time takes around half of all working age males, and 15 per cent of working age females to southern Ghana for periods of at least a year.[112] Similarly, the World Bank Voices of the Poor report on Ghana argues that urban and rural young people feel they have no choice but to leave home in search of work, since their remittances are likely to make the difference between food security or a lack of food security for their families.[113] In the

Upper East region in particular, infertile soils and lack of local services are seen as contributing to out-migration. Meanwhile a recent PhD study by Mensah-Bonsu suggests that over half of rural outmigration in northeast Ghana is for work reasons, and that this is dominated by movement to other rural areas.[114] This study also suggests that migration is a phenomenon mainly involving young people, where permanent migration is often preceded by short-term seasonal migration.

However, it is also worth noting that for Ghana as a whole, as reported in the GLSS, 60 per cent of migrants reported marriage or other family reasons as the cause of their migration, with only 25 per cent reporting work reasons. This was partly because the GLSS includes as migrants not just household heads, but members of the family aged over 15 who moved with them, and also return migrants who might be less likely to move for employment reasons. Nonetheless, if these two categories are excluded, still only 40 per cent of migrant household heads were found to have moved for employment, with the majority citing other reasons.

The impacts of migration on the poor, and on poor regions, are the subject of some dispute. Some work suggests that it may be the poorest groups in northern villages who benefit most from remittances, rather than the middle and 'secure' groups.[115] A fairly optimistic picture is also painted by a recent analysis of GLSS data, which found a 'migration premium' in that migrants had statistically higher living standards than non-migrants, although this premium had declined by a half between surveys in 1991/92 and 1998/99.[116] It is difficult, however, in such analysis, to separate out cause and effect – in other words, it may simply be the less poor who are more able to migrate, rather than that migration makes people less poor.

In contrast, Cleveland's study of the Upper East region found that migration increased dependency ratios (the number of young and elderly dependent on each working age adult) in sending areas, and that remittances and improvements in land and labour productivity were insufficient to compensate for this increased dependency.[117] Mensah-Bonsu found migrants send home only US$5-15 a year in remittances, making litttle impact on rural livelihoods.[118] Meanwhile, even if internal remittances do appear to redistribute some wealth from rich to poor regions, this effect may not be sustainable in the face of the decline of the cocoa industry.

There has been some forced migration within Ghana: e.g. from 1994-95, around 100,000 people are estimated to have been uprooted in northern Ghana as a result of ethnic conflict over land, of whom 10,000 moved to neighbouring Togo. Although most returned as the conflict subsided, some remain displaced.

Over the last decade, academic and media attention on internal migration of the poor in Ghana has tended to move away from north-south migration in general to more specific issues, such as the link between migration and HIV/AIDS, and an apparently growing number of women and especially child migrants who may be victims of trafficking and/or other exploitative practices. The proliferation of HIV/AIDS is said to be linked to the movement of women from rural to urban areas where they do not earn enough to live, and where they are therefore exposed to prostitution, rape, and/or promiscuity.[119] Having contacted HIV, they are then said to return to their villages where they infect men with whom they come into contact. However, it is also worth noting that a study of Ghanaian women working Abidjan found that those selling sex – some 75 per cent of the sample – were earning between six and seven times the national minimum wage in Ghana, irrespective of their level of education and skills.[120] Such work was regarded by many women as a successful short-term livelihood strategy.

There is also concern about trafficking, such as children sold by their parents to fishermen on Lake Volta, or adolescent girls working as porters ('kayayee') at lorry stations and markets in Accra and Kumasi. Examples have also been cited of children being handed over to women by parents on the understanding that they will be sent to school, given training, or taken care of within a household, but instead the children are put into paid work and no money is given to the child or the parent (see Box 6). Most trafficked children are believed to be from the Northern region, the eastern part of Greater Accra, and from the peripheral and urban slum areas around Accra. Sekondo-Takoradi, the capital of Western region, is also said to be a major recruiting centre and thoroughfare for internationally trafficked children.[121] The Ghana Immigration Service estimates that 3,582 women were trafficked between 1998-2000, and IOM returned 535 trafficked women to neighbouring countries in 1999-2000. However, detailed data on child trafficking is not available.

2.6.3 International Migration and the Brain Drain

Substantial numbers of Ghanaians have left the country since the 1970s to work and/or study in both Europe and North America. As with many West African countries, it is difficult to find accurate statistics, as undocumented migration is thought to make up a fair proportion of total migration. It has been estimated that in 1996, there were 31,000 Ghanaians in the UK[122], whilst in 2001, over 100,000 Ghanaians were thought to be in each of the US and Canada.[123] Ghanaians also appear to be particularly spread around the world, with deportations of Ghanaians occurring from some 58 different countries in 1998.[124]

Attitudes towards this international migration have been somewhat divided, with concern expressed by many observers about the brain drain, but also a growing level of interest in the potential for remittances and returnees to contribute to national development (see Box 7). Ghana is estimated to have lost around 14,000 teachers between 1975 and 1981 – many of them to Nigeria.[125] The proportion of health workers leaving Ghana has reached quite dramatic proportions in recent years (Table 6), stimulating considerable media attention and calls for measures to stem the flow.

However, at the same time, the media have also focused on the transfer of money to Ghana by its nationals abroad[126], with inward remittances estimated in one report at $1.5 billion for January-September 2003 alone.[127] This estimate dwarfs a previous Bank of Ghana estimate for 2001 of around $400 million in migrant remittances, which even then was the equivalent of 20 per cent of Ghana's export earnings; both are an order of magnitude higher than the official IMF figure for workers' remittances which stood at $32 million in 2000.[128] Another recent study suggested that professionals outside Ghana each remit between $1,000 and $5,000 annually, with a mean of $2,200.[129] There appears to have been a mushrooming of both formal and informal money transfer outlets to process such transfers.

Box 7: International migration and development in Ghana

A recent special issue of the journal *Population, Place and Space* devoted to migration and return in West Africa includes three articles that focus on the impact of migration, return and remittances on Ghana, two of which were based on a recent DFID-funded survey of return to the country. One shows how, amongst less-skilled returnees to both Ghana and neighbouring Côte d'Ivoire, families have a significant impact on migration patterns, with those whose migration formed part of a family strategy being two and a half times more likely to return with savings over $10,000.

Elite returnees to the two countries were found to have brought with them concrete innovative practices and productive investments.

A third contribution, focused on Ghana alone, shows how remittances from Netherlands-based emigrants have also had a significant impact on families and community development back home, although this impact varies and can be highly insecure.

Source: Population, Space and Place, 10(2), (2004)

Table 6: Proportion of health workers leaving Ghana as percentage of those trained that year									
Profession	1995	1996	1997	1998	1999	2000	2001	2002	1995-2002
GPs/Medical officers									
Trained	93	104	84	85	113	84	67	72	702
Emigrated	56	68	59	58	68	50	60	68	487
% leaving	60.2	5.4	70.2	68.2	60.2	59.5	89.6	94.4	69.4
Dentists									
Trained	10	13	9	9	12	9	7	8	77
Emigrated	2	3	3	3	4	2	2	2	21
% leaving	20	23.1	33.3	33.3	33.3	22.2	28.6	25	27.3
Pharmacists									
Trained	67	65	80	120	120	120	120	120	812
Emigrated	29	27	35	53	49	24	58	77	352
% leaving	43.3	41.5	43.8	44.2	40.8	20	48.3	64.2	43.3
Medical laboratory technologists/ technicians									
Trained	31	37	38	45	46	46	45	51	339
Emigrated	8	9	4	6	9	16	14	0	66
% leaving	25.8	24.3	10.5	13.3	19.6	34.8	31.1	0	19.5
Environmental health specialists									
Trained	0	0	1	0	0	0	0	0	1
Emigrated	0	0	0	0	1	0	0	0	1
% leaving	na	na	0	na	na	na	na	na	100
Environmental health technolo-gists/technicians									
Trained	100	112	108	109	139	145	135	144	992
Emigrated	2	6	6	3	3	0	2	3	25
% leaving	2	5.4	5.6	2.8	2.2	0	1.5	2.1	2.5
Nurses/midwives									
Trained	975	911	868	814	1073	1037	1124	1074	7876
Emigrated	195	182	174	161	215	207	205	214	1553
% leaving	20	20	20	19.8	20	20	18.2	19.9	19.7
Total									
Trained	1276	1242	1188	1182	1503	1441	1498	1469	10799
Emigrated	292	295	281	284	349	299	341	364	2505
% leaving	22.9	23.8	23.7	24	23.2	20.7	22.8	24.8	23.2
Source: ISSER (2003) State of the Ghana Economy									

2.6.4 Migration Policies

Migration policies in Ghana are currently focused on limiting the departure of skilled migrants, and encouraging those abroad to return. Dual citizenship has been extended to Ghanaians living abroad as an encouragement for them to return freely. The National Patriotic Party has made a conscious effort to strengthen relations with diaspora communities and associations. A Non-Resident Ghanaians Secretariat (NRGS) was established in May 2003 to link with Ghanaians abroad and encourage return, whilst a Homecoming Summit was organised by the government in 2001.[130]

On brain drain in the health sector, President Kufour has pledged the government's determination to offer resources and support to the Council of Ghana College of Physicians and Surgeons in their effort to stop the brain drain.[131] Measures have been taken to address the issue through improved working conditions in the health sector, including the provision of cars to health sector workers, although there have been complaints that these have gone exclusively to doctors rather than nurses, leading to resentment and an apparent increased desire to emigrate amongst nurses.[132]

There is also recognition in Ghana that the exodus of health personnel reflects a lack of opportunities for professional development inside Ghana. In response, the Ghana Information Network for Knowledge Sharing (GINKS), an NGO, is seeking to provide continuous medical education through newsletters, CD-Roms and the internet. The Ministry of Health is discussing with the World Bank and Howard University ways of implementing the use of 'tele-medicine' in Ghana.

Ghana is a signatory to both the refugee and migrant worker conventions, but has not ratified the 2000 protocols on trafficking and smuggling. In 1998, the Ghanaian Parliament approved a comprehensive Children's Act, which prohibits work by children under 15, whilst it adopted the ILO Convention on the Worst Forms of Child Labour in 2000. IOM launched a programme in 2001 for the return and reintegration of children trafficked to Central and Volta regions, which includes measures to offer business advice and loans for small enterprises to parents who sold their children to fishing communities on Lake Volta.

There is also considerable NGO activity on child trafficking to and within Ghana. World Vision International works to reduce rural-urban migration and prevent young people from 'drifting' to the cities, whilst Catholic Action for Street Children works to improve the lives of street children and promote their rights through child sponsorship. Other agencies have launched initiatives to return children to their home villages in northern Ghana, although the children themselves have not always welcomed these measures.

Ghana does appear to have begun to grapple with some of the impacts of migration on development and poverty reduction, with policy development focusing at present on stemming the brain drain (especially in the health sector), reaching out to Ghanaians abroad, and addressing the problem of child trafficking. As Ghana's economy improves, it is likely that the country will need to deal increasingly with issues of immigration and the return of its nationals, rather than addressing the loss of Ghanaians overseas.

However, as with Nigeria, perhaps the key policy gap is not so much international migration as addressing patterns of internal migration and their impact on poverty. In Ghana, these patterns are especially complex, as rural-rural migration and movements from towns back to rural areas continue to feature strongly in contemporary movements, even if regions of destination may be changing. The government's anti-poverty plans, as set out in the PRSP, do not as yet take this migration into account.

A particularly poorly understood area is that of the migration of children, whose movement is often characterised as forced, but in which the reality may again be somewhat more complex.

2.7 Sierra Leone and Liberia

2.7.1 Introduction

Like Nigeria and Ghana, Sierra Leone and Liberia have also historically been countries of immigration, but now have substantial numbers of nationals living abroad as a result of economic and political collapse. Yet, to a much greater degree than in most neighbouring countries, the key migration issues relate to forced migration. Over the last decade, Sierra Leone and Liberia have experienced a huge amount of displacement of their populations. The 11-year civil war in Sierra Leone is estimated to have caused the displacement of between one and three million people. Although internal displacement is now officially at an end, many certainly remain in host areas. In Liberia, conflict from 1989-96 displaced as much as two thirds of the population and numbers of IDPs at the present time are estimated to be around 140,000.[133]

Displaced people in the two countries come in at least three distinct categories. First, up to a quarter of a million officially registered IDPs in Sierra Leone
have been returned to their places of origin since the end of the war under
the auspices of the government's Resettlement Strategy. Although benefiting
from a settlement package, which included a two-month food ration, household utensils, plastic sheeting, and in some cases transportation, conditions in
home areas often remain difficult, and the process has been criticised in some
quarters for not being entirely voluntary. A similar process, and similar criti-
cisms about the degree of voluntariness of resettlement, apply in Liberia.

Second, clearly there is a large discrepancy between the number of IDPs
that have returned in Sierra Leone, and estimates of the total number of IDPs
at the height of the conflict. In part, this is accounted for by 'spontaneous'
return, without assistance, but there are also many who were displaced, but
were never officially registered with the authorities, or were de-registered, and
have not since been resettled. This group can be seen as representing a quasi-
permanent rural-urban migration flow of some magnitude.

Third, there has also been international movement of refugees. There were
over half a million Sierra Leoneans in neighbouring countries, especially
Guinea, at the height of the war in the mid-1990s, and an estimated 135,000
in 2003, with on-going returns from the two main destinations, Guinea and
Liberia. There remain over 270,000 Liberians living as refugees mainly in
Guinea – to which new flows occurred in 2002 – and Côte d'Ivoire, from which
there has been some recent repatriation as a result of the spread of conflict to
that country.

Although migration primarily means forced displacement in Sierra Leone and
Liberia, it is important not to ignore other types of mobility. In Sierra Leone,
there have long been movements from rural areas to towns. Yet post-conflict
Sierra Leone is characterised by a resurgence of localised identities, built
around village registration as the cornerstone of citizenship and access to basic
rights, property and protection.[134] As a result, continued mobility within the
country may serve to exclude migrants from such rights: e.g. people remaining
as 'squatters' in Freetown are likely to be excluded in this way.

2.7.2 Importance of Migration to the Poor

According to the UN's Human Development Index 2003, Sierra Leone continues to be the poorest country in the world. The last household survey conducted in Sierra Leone was in 1989/90, prior to the civil war. At this stage,

poverty was already 'endemic and pervasive'. Life expectancy at birth is now estimated to stand at 34.5 years and adult literacy at 36 per cent.[135] GDP per capita in US dollars fell by 35 per cent between 1990 and 2000. Primary school net enrolment fell from 55 per cent in 1990 to 42 per cent in 1999, in part because of the displacement of teachers. A total of 57 per cent of Sierra Leone's population fall below the $1 a day poverty line, although this is lower than a number of neighbouring countries, including Nigeria. Lower levels of income poverty notwithstanding, these indicators highlight the extent of poverty that prevails in Sierra Leone, and point to the role played by conflict and displacement in increasing the incidence, depth and severity of this poverty.

However, internal migration in both Sierra Leone and Liberia certainly predates the most recent conflicts. In Sierra Leone, circular rural-rural migrations have long been directed to the main swamp rice-growing areas of Cambia district in the North and Bonthe district in the South, as well as the main cash-cropping districts of the East and the diamond mining areas of the South and East, whilst there was also substantial movement out of rural areas to urban centres of employment.[136] There have also historically been substantial movements to the Firestone rubber plantation in Liberia. Although the latter is largely abandoned at present, a recent study of the diamond mining areas in Sierra Leone suggests the migration of perhaps 10,000 seasonal workers may still support 70,000 or more poor people in sending districts.[137]

A study of the role of internal remittances sent by a sample of 1,500 rural out-migrants in Sierra Leone in 1981-82 found that remittances on average comprised only 12 per cent of the incomes of rural households. Yet this rose to over 40 per cent of the income of the poorest households, with their overall effect being to reduce income inequality in poor areas.[138] In turn, although remittances were mainly used in rural areas for consumption, about 16 per cent were used for building or house improvement, whilst 6 per cent were used to set up and/or improve export crop plantations in rural areas.[139]

More recent studies on internal migration for work, or on IDPs who have chosen not to return to their home area, are not available for either country. One useful source of information in Sierra Leone may be a new National Household Income and Expenditure Survey, although continued insecurity means there is no equivalent for Liberia.

2.7.3 International Migration and the Brain Drain

It is unclear exactly how many Sierra Leoneans and Liberians live abroad, but as noted above, over 20,000 people born in Sierra Leone were counted in the 2000 US census. There are also believed to be considerable numbers of Liberians in the US, many still holding a form of 'temporary protection'. International migration between Liberia and Sierra Leone and western countries also has a long history, dating in the Liberian case to that country's colonisation by freed slaves from the Americas. The movement of men from Liberia and Sierra Leone as stevedores and seafarers not only to other West African ports, but also to Britain and Europe, also dates to the nineteenth century.[140]

Although less studied than Ghanaian and Nigerian associations, there is some evidence that Sierra Leoneans and Liberians abroad have played a role in peace-building and development in their home countries. At the height of the civil war in Liberia, the Liberian Islamic Union for Relief and Development (LIURD), a major NGO that provided assistance to displaced and war-affected populations in the West of Liberia, was established through the efforts of expatriate Liberians living in Philadelphia in the US. More recently, the Coalition of Concerned Liberians (CCL) was established in Washington, DC to represent various Liberian humanitarian groups and lobby for increased US involvement in Liberia.

There are numerous Sierra Leonean organisations in the UK and North America. One example is the 'Sierra Leonean Women's Forum' in the UK, which although primarily orientated to providing advice, information, assistance and social events for Sierra Leonean women in the UK, also raises funds for food and clothing to be sent to Sierra Leone, and promotes awareness of gender and development issues in Sierra Leone.

2.7.4 Migration Policies

The Sierra Leone Interim Poverty Reduction Strategy Paper (I-PRSP) consists of three central pillars: improved governance, revival of economic growth and extension of social services. However, whilst it mentions the challenges faced in the resettlement of displaced people, and highlights policies to supply returnees to farming areas with agricultural seeds, tools and services to improve food security, and encourages artisanal miners returning to mining areas to form cooperatives, consideration of migration is otherwise largely absent.[141]

A lack of attention to migration is also characteristic of policy elsewhere.

One example is a Community Reintegration and Rehabilitation Project (CRRP), funded by the World Bank and ADB, and launched in 2000, which seeks to address the short-term needs of ex-combatants, IDPs, returnees, and the communities to which they are returning. The project locates these needs in the context of remaining in rural areas, and not re-opening previous channels of migration. This is despite heavy investment in road-building that might stimulate renewed mobility.

One exception involves the National Long Term Perspectives Study (NLTPS) Vision 2025 Programme being developed by the Sierra Leone government with UNDP assistance. This study has created a website to solicit the views of Sierra Leoneans in the diaspora.[142] The Sierra Leone government has also organised a series of 'Homecoming Summits', the latest of which was held in Freetown in December 2003.[143]

In relation to trafficking, the Sierra Leonean government is not seen by the US State Department as fully complying with the minimum standards for the elimination of trafficking, although it considers that the government is making significant effort to do so. There are no specific laws against trafficking but there are laws against 'procuring a female by threats or coercion for the purpose of prostitution'.[144] The Mano River Union countries (Liberia, Sierra Leone and Guinea) have also formed the Mano River Human Rights Network to address specific human rights issues in each of the countries.[145]

In Liberia, there is as yet no PRSP, and the country and government are currently arguably too unstable for clear policies on migration to have developed, although there are signs already that the new government is interested in promoting the return of exiles from the US.

As both Liberia and Sierra Leone move towards a more sustainable peace, the key issue relating to migration is clearly the return of refugees and displaced persons, rather than migration for economic reasons. Within Sierra Leone in particular, there have been efforts to build local institutional structures to manage local development, whilst in both countries there has been direct material assistance to returnees.

However, internationally, it is worth noting that the UK is moving ahead with a refugee resettlement programme to move up to 500 Liberian, Ivorian or possibly Sierra Leonean refugees currently registered in Accra to new homes in the UK. Although targeted at 'old case load' refugees, this could be seen as giving mixed signals at a time when the emphasis is on return.

It is also important to bear in mind that in the context of disrupted livelihood opportunities and continued insecurity in rural Liberia and Sierra Leone, the option of diversification of livelihoods through migration is likely to remain an attractive one for many individuals and families. Policies to promote sustainable rural development and peace-building need to avoid 'trapping' families in rural areas, based on a misconception that their full-time presence there is a precondition for peace and development. Rather, increased attention could be paid to the benefits of strong interactions between rural and urban areas.

Chapter

3 MIGRATION & DEVELOPMENT IN EAST AFRICA

3.1 Overview

- East Africa has a long history of labour migration between and within countries to plantations (cotton and coffee in Uganda), mines (DRC and Uganda) and with the seasons (pastoralist communities in Uganda, Tanzania and Kenya). In the post-colonial era, these movements have been supplemented by substantial forced displacement, and increasing rural-urban migration within countries for employment or to earn a livelihood. However, both urbanization rates and levels of international migration remain generally lower than in other parts of Africa.

- Labour circulation forms a particularly important part of migration within East Africa, although the region has also witnessed substantial movements of refugees and internally displaced people, which have affected virtually every country in the region. In particular, Tanzania, Kenya and Uganda all remain host to substantial refugee populations.

- In contrast, international migration is relatively weak in the region, with the exception of the Horn of Africa, which has seen substantial movement to the US (from Ethiopia and Somalia), Europe (from Somalia) and the Middle East (from Somalia and Sudan).

- A range of innovative informal remittance systems have developed across the region to facilitate especially intra-country flows through bus and courier companies, and in the case of Somalia, substantial flows from overseas. However, there is some evidence that trust in internal remittance systems at least is eroding, whilst Somali money transfer agencies have raised some regulatory concerns.

- Empirical studies of the impact of migration on poverty and poor people are relatively rich in East Africa, and can contribute to understanding of how pro-poor policy can take migration into account. Yet despite this empirical knowledge base, and attempts to foster regional integration, attitudes towards both migration and refugee flows appear sceptical at least, and probably have hardened in recent years.

- The extent to which rural households engage in short- and long-term migration to maintain and diversify household income and reduce risk in the face of agro-climatic constraints is relatively well documented in East Africa. Studies have shown that rural families increase their livelihood security by splitting the locations of the family. Research in Western Kenya suggests that the decision to migrate, and remittance behaviour, are linked to a form of intergenerational 'migration contract' between a migrant and his or her parents, in which the (usually male) migrant moves and sends remittances in expectation of a subsequent inheritance. In southern Tanzania, research by IIED suggests that male migration to save and invest in rural areas is also common, although return is less so. In contrast, in northern Tanzania, opportunities for migration appear to be especially important for marginalised women.

- An interesting feature of East African migration is the circulation of children in order to obtain education. Although helping to build national rather than ethnic identity, migration for education means that secondary school pupils can circulate each term over very large distances. It may also encourage onward migration once schooling is completed. Yet education also appears to be a major focus of the community, and remittances are often invested in school fees. Those who have educated relatives in urban areas also appear to receive larger remittances and are therefore able to send a higher proportion of their children to school, perpetuating inequality from one generation to the next.

- There are a number of key knowledge gaps concerning migration and displacement within and from East Africa:

  - Although useful research exists, there remains a need for deeper understanding of the relationships between migration and development in the region, including estimates of the scale of internal migration and its impact on rural livelihoods. In most countries in East Africa, recent survey data on internal migration that is nationally representative is simply unavailable.

  - The lack of reliable estimates of the numbers of East Africans living abroad, their economic contribution to East African countries, and the effect of their exodus on availability of skilled professionals in sectors such as health and education, may explain why international migration flows appear low across the region. Particular attention may need to be paid to migration to South Africa and the Gulf.

- Understanding of the significance and socio-economic impact of immigration into East African countries, including that of temporary workers and refugees, is also a priority. Such understanding could contribute to a more informed policy debate in the face of proposals to limit migration (as recently in Kenya) or to adopt a more restrictive stance towards refugees (as recently in Tanzania).

- The extent of the turnaround in policy on emigration from Uganda is quite substantial, and reflects the new goal of the Ugandan Government to develop the potential economic contribution of the diaspora, rather than encouraging them not to leave. This could form a model for other countries in the region, although for some countries, conflict resolution and the rebuilding of failed states is clearly a more urgent priority.

- In Uganda, the liberalisation of financial markets, especially trade in foreign exchange, and the granting of permission for foreign denominated bank accounts, are said to have increased remittances. The Bank of Uganda Forex and Trade Department is now generally supportive and positively inclined towards granting permission to Money Transfer Organisations (MTOs). There is also some interest in using Micro-Finance Institutions (MFIs) as providers of money transfer services, and evidence across the region suggests that these may be more effective in channelling resources to the poorest than international banks and corporations that lack local knowledge.

3.2 Region-Wide Issues

Like West Africa, East Africa has a long history of labour migration between and within countries to plantations (cotton and coffee in Uganda), mines (DRC and Uganda) and with the seasons (pastoralist communities in Uganda, Tanzania and Kenya). In the colonial era, labour migration was orientated mainly from Rwanda, Burundi and Zaire to Uganda, Kenya and Tanzania, as well as more recently from Sudan and the Horn of Africa to the Middle East.[146] There is also a history of rural-urban migration within countries for employment or to earn a livelihood, although urbanization rates remain generally lower than in much of West or Southern Africa.

Box 8: Migration and education

One interesting feature of East African migration is the circulation of children in order to obtain education. Such flows have historical precedents in the pre-colonial and colonial education systems, and form an important part of mobility within Kenya, Tanzania and Uganda. These patterns were maintained at least until the 1980s, despite greater availability of schools within daily commuting distance.

For example, the national admission systems to secondary schools in all three countries mean that pupils can be allocated places in schools anywhere in the country, some of which are boarding schools and others of which are not. This system, created to encourage the building of a national rather than ethnic identity, means that secondary school pupils can circulate each term over very large distances.

Migration for education may also encourage onward migration once schooling is completed. The greater availability of formal sector jobs in towns, and higher wages available there, are also relevant factors.

Sources: Gould (1985); see endnote 147.

A major focus of literature on migration flows and processes in East Africa is circulation. This process of temporary or semi-permanent migration from a rural area to another rural or an urban area for employment is characterised by the links maintained with the area of origin. These circulation patterns have strong historical roots in East Africa: e.g. in Buganda, before colonisation, it was traditional to send young men to live and work with other relatives for some years in order to gain a better understanding of Bugandan culture.[147] There has also been substantial movement of pastoralists.[148]

Colonial labour laws enforced patterns of circulatory migration. They divided the areas of production and reproduction, moving African families into labour reserves, from which men were recruited to work in cities or on plantations. The rest of a family had to remain in the reserves, subsisting on crops grown in the area without the help of the most active members of the family. In this context, cash remittances from family members working in the colonial economy assumed considerable importance.[149]

Since the 1980s, labour circulation has decreased and refugee flows have started to dominate movement.[150] According to the IOM Migration Policy Framework for sub-Saharan Africa:

> This subregion has been, and is, experiencing movements of refugees and internally displaced persons (IDPs) ... Much of the

voluntary migration that characterised the Eastern African Community (EAC) countries of Kenya, Tanzania and Uganda ceased by 1978 and has never resurfaced in the resuscitated Economic Community of Central African States (CEAC) (since 1996). Countries in the sub-region do not have explicit policies on migration and no sub-regional cooperation mechanism to respond to their common migration challenges.

On rural-urban migration, it has been argued that following economic decline and the impacts of structural adjustment programmes in the 1980s, the real incomes of a large proportion of the urban population declined dramatically.[151] As a result, urban growth has slowed considerably in countries such as Tanzania, Uganda and Zambia, giving way to return migration to rural areas in some cases. Nonetheless, out-migration continues, notably movement to the Gulf.[152]

Table 7: Selected development and migration indicators for East African countries					
Country	Population (millions) 2000	GDP per capita (US$ PPP) 2000	Human Development Index (HDI) 2000	Migrant stock (%) 2000	Average annual net migration rate (per 1000) 1995-2000
Angola	13.1	2187	0.403	0.4	-1.4
Burundi	6.3	591	0.313	1.2	-12.9
Djibouti	0.6	2377	0.445	4.5	6.8
DR Congo	50.9	765	0.431	1.5	-7.1
Eritrea	3.7	837	0.421	0.4	0.6
Ethiopia	62.9	668	0.327	1.0	-0.1
Kenya	30.7	1022	0.513	1.1	-0.1
Rwanda	7.6	943	0.403	1.2	62.8
Somalia	8.8	795*	0.284*	0.2	-0.6
Sudan	31.1	1797	0.499	2.5	-2.6
Tanzania	35.1	522	0.440	2.5	-1.4
Uganda	23.3	1208	0.444	2.3	-0.6
Source: Figures compiled from UNDP and UN Population Division. For notes on terms, see Table 2. * Somali figures are for 2001					

A number of key themes emerge in relation to migration in the East African region, including:

- The importance of circulation, building on historic patterns of labour migration from rural areas to towns and cities and to areas of mining and plantation agriculture;

- The development of a range of informal remittance systems that have transferred money both within countries, and more recently from international migrants (see Box 9), although trust in these systems is eroding in some cases (see Box 12);

- A degree of regional integration that has fostered mobility between East African countries (see Boxes 10 and 15);

- For Kenya, Tanzania and Uganda, the existence of a number of empirical studies of the use of migrant remittances by the poor (see Box 11), which could contribute to understanding of how pro-poor policy could take migration into account;

- Despite this empirical base of knowledge, continuing worries about the negative consequences of migration on the part of a number of key policy-makers in the region, although the Ugandan government appears to have developed a more positive attitude towards linking with the diaspora (see Box 13); and

- The rising significance of forced migration (including internal displacement – see Box 14), although more recently this has given way to substantial return of refugees and IDPs in some countries.

In this section, in addition to a broad overview, we focus on particular studies in Sudan and the Horn of Africa. Work on Tanzania, Kenya, Rwanda and Uganda is then considered in more detail in subsequent country sections.

3.2 Importance of Migration to the Poor

Migration is of considerable importance to the poor in East Africa. Historically, the migration of millions of rural households in eastern and southern Africa has provided investment capital for rural commodity production, stimulated the flow of new ideas and social practices into rural areas, and enhanced rural livelihoods.[153] Decreasing agricultural incomes across East Africa since the 1970s have led to a diversification of livelihood sources, and migration is a likely outcome in areas with easy access to labour markets.[154] The impact of urban economic decline has also been felt by the poor, although many public sector workers previously considered to be amongst the 'labour aristocracy' have perhaps been hardest hit.

In Ethiopia, interesting information on the relationship between migration and poverty is available from work on livelihoods. This has shown that the poor migrate more than the better off, in order to supplement income from the land, and repay or avoid incurring debts.[155] Although permanent or semi-permanent migration was seen by most families as an option of last resort, temporary seasonal migrations were often actively encouraged as a right of passage for young men. However, it is those with some assets, rather than none, who were found most able to migrate.

Migration may affect the poor, but the impact of migration on poverty is more difficult to determine.[156] Thus, although migration plays a central role in the livelihoods of rural households and communities, rich and poor, it was found that migration may increase inequality. The research also did not produce comparable quantitative estimates of the impact of migration on livelihoods. In fact, one of the lessons learned was that it was difficult to generalise about this. In policy terms, particularly, it was seen to be important to be aware of specific contexts in order that policies could be as supportive as possible.

A study of female Ethiopian migrants to the Middle East also showed that many women are trafficked to destinations outside Ethiopia and are left in vulnerable positions, partly due to the strict laws surrounding the migration of women.[157] When in the Middle East, most of the women work as maids or nannies, in jobs with little security or protection. The report partially blames the patriarchal Ethiopian society and the lack of education and career opportunities for women within Ethiopia as a cause of these exploitative forms of migration.

Box 9: Informal remittance systems

Recent estimates suggest that Somali money transfer companies deal with approximately $750 million in transfers to the country each year, yet these systems are largely 'informal' in comparison with western banks.

Somali remittance companies utilise the 'Hawalla' system, which relies on trust and ethnic bonds to transfer money around the world.

Initially unregulated, concerns over the need for financial regulation have been raised in response to accusations of money laundering and links to Al Qaida following the September 11th attacks. As a result, the Somali Financial Services Association (SFSA) was launched in 2003.

In Somalia, it is international migration that has received most attention, not least because of the collapse of the state and with it virtually all social science research within the country. Somalis have moved in large numbers to Europe and North America, and in the US at least, census data shows that Somalis are less educated than any other African nationality, and indeed the only African country of origin where educational levels are below the US national average. However, interestingly, Somali international migrants have remitted quite large sums to the country even in the absence of a formal banking system (see Box 9).

In other East African countries there are further examples of innovative formal and informal mechanisms to transfer remittances, including the use of bus and courier companies.[158] Another innovative semi-formal system, although not actually a money transfer system, which has sprung up in Uganda and Tanzania, is the transfer of pre-paid airtime on mobile phones to relatives (via passing on the pin code). This saves the relatives money in buying airtime and allows them to use it for other expenses.

3.4 International Migration and the Brain Drain

International migration from Somalia may have brought substantial remittances, but in most other countries of the region it is seen as a major problem because of the 'brain drain'. In Ethiopia, it has been estimated that between a quarter and three quarters of students and professionals travelling abroad to study have not returned to Ethiopia, with a particular loss to the academic and medical professions.[159] Indeed, Ethiopia has the largest number of nationals of any East African nation in the US, and the second largest in Africa after Nigeria. By 1995, it was estimated that some 500,000 skilled Sudanese were working abroad.[160]

There has also been some circulation of professionals within East Africa, not all of it voluntary (e.g. Kenya and Tanzania benefited from the immigration of professionals from Uganda during the Amin era).

3.5 Migration Policies

An International Migration Policy Conference for East Africa, the Horn of Africa and the Great Lakes Region, was held in Nairobi, Kenya in May 2002, and brought together 170 high, senior and middle level government officials from

Burundi, Djibouti, Democratic Republic of Congo, Eritrea, Ethiopia, Kenya, Rwanda, Sudan, Uganda, Tanzania and Yemen. The Conference, believed to be the first of its kind in the region, identified a series of migration and forced displacement issues of interest and concern, including:

- Forced displacement (refugee protection and asylum; regional processing of secondary migratory movements; IDP access and assistance; mobility and human security; protracted displacement situations; migration, forced displacement and conflict resolution; crisis prevention and conflict resolution; and media sensitisation to issues of displacement and as a tool for awareness raising);

- The management of labour migration (maximising remittances; pre-departure training; bilateral agreements to avoid double taxation; monitoring circular migration; brain drain; registration and supervision of foreign employment agencies; ensuring migrant workers' rights at home and abroad; integration and re-integration; strengthening co-operation with African diasporas; matching labour needs and demand; and facilitating exchange of knowledge, skills and resources);

- The establishment of a Strategic Framework for an Integrated Policy on Migration on the African Continent (including partnerships between African countries and the EU; and inter-State dialogue and co-operation concerning return, readmission and re-integration).

With respect to labour migration, a number of policy initiatives can be highlighted across the region. There are regional initiatives to promote free movement in the East African Community (see Box 10) and COMESA countries also plan to establish gradually the free movement of citizens as part of the creation of a free trade area, although there have been few signs of progress so far.[161]

ILO has a sectoral programme on the elimination of the worst forms of child labour in the commercial agriculture sector in East Africa, working with the governments of Kenya, Tanzania, Uganda, Malawi and Zambia and funded by the US Department of Labor. There has recently been a mid-term evaluation of this programme.

In addition, IOM's MIDA project has also made greater strides in East Africa than elsewhere in the continent, with one initiative aiming to build the capacity of the governments of Kenya, Tanzania and Uganda to provide protection to their citizens working abroad and to expand legal labour migration opportunities for the benefit and development of their countries of origin.

However, measures to promote freer movement have not received universal acclaim, and in some cases, policies have worked in the opposite direction.

> ## Box 10: Regional passports
>
> The EAC has also recently introduced new 'East African passports' and temporary passes to speed up movement between countries in the region, as well as abolishing charges on the temporary importation of private vehicles across regional borders, and establishing special immigration counters for East African travelers at the region's airports. The passports cost US$10 and have six months' multiple entry validity. New policies are also being considered on the application of national status treatment to East African nationals in any of the Partner States with respect to access to services in the fields of health, education and training, tourism and communications, among others.
>
> *Source: EAC Information and Publications Office*

In Ethiopia, the ADB has awarded $86 million in loans and grants in order to control what it sees as a massive explosion in rural to urban migration. This will be used for investments in rural areas, such as infrastructure development and credit facilities for rural farmers in an attempt to increase rural enterprise and prevent people having to move to the cities.[162]

In the case of the EAC, the issue of labour migration has met resistance from some member states because of the different levels of advancement in training of human resources in the three countries.[163] Thus whilst Kenya enrols about 45,000 students in its institutions of higher learning, Uganda admits only 20,000 and Tanzania just 7,000, leading to fears in the latter two countries that Kenyans will flood their job markets and render citizens of their countries jobless.

At a recent conference, Uganda's Minister of State responsible for Gender, Labour and Social Development, Henry Joseph Obbo, commented that the harmonisation of labour laws, labour migration and free movement of persons needed to take into account the aspect of the level of training in each country, although Kenya's Minister for Labour and Human Resources Development, Ali Chirau Mwakwere, expressed reservations in turn about Pakistanis who had 'flooded' the Kenyan job market while many Kenyans were jobless.

In relation to forced migration, there have also been efforts to develop a regional set of policies. In April 2002, a consortium of NGOs hosted a regional meeting in Mombasa that sought to promote a 'progressive legislative and policy framework' across the region.[164] At a subsequent meeting in Dar-es-Salaam in September 2003, Tanzania proposed the introduction of a policy of 'safe havens' in conflict-ridden countries as a way of averting large-scale refugee movements, as well as regional burden sharing arrangements, whilst Zambia proposed the introduction of measures to allow refugees to become economic players in the host country, therefore reducing the burden on the host.[165] Although this conference, which brought together representatives from Burundi, the Democratic Republic of Congo, Kenya, Malawi, Rwanda, Tanzania, Uganda, Zambia, UNHCR and the AU, failed to reach agreement on these proposals, governments did recommit to the principle of refugee protection in the region.

Large-scale displacement from Somalia, Ethiopia, Sudan, Rwanda, Burundi and the DRC has made this region a key area for discussion of policies on refugees and IDPs. Historically, Tanzania had one of the most progressive pieces of refugee legislation in the world, although state practice has become much more restrictive since the presence of over a million Rwandans in the country from 1994-96. It is reassuring that the notion of a 'progressive' policy on forced migration is now on the agenda, along with regional passports and free movement of workers, even if these still raise problems for some in government.

However, although dealing with forced displacement continues to be an important issue in the region, it is not unreasonable to expect that the return of refugees and IDPs might gain increasing importance in the coming years. After large-scale returns to Rwanda in late 1996, there have been some returns at least to countries such as Angola, Burundi, Ethiopia, Uganda, and Somaliland. Here, it is clearly important for countries (and refugee agencies) to learn from experience in different countries about what kind of assistance is needed by returnees, and the most appropriate policies to promote an economic, political and social environment in which return can have positive outcomes.

As elsewhere on the continent, it is probably internal migration that is most significant for the poor in most countries, and where policy gaps are therefore most conspicuous. This issue is considered in more depth below, in relation to four specific East African countries, Kenya, Tanzania, Uganda and Rwanda.

3.6 Kenya

3.6.1 Introduction

According to a recent review of international migration from Kenya in 2001 there were 47,000 Kenyan nationals in the US, 20,600 in Canada and 15,000 in the UK.[166] In the 1980s and 1990s, this appears increasingly to reflect permanent, rather than circular migration, due to the political and economic instability in Kenya. Many workers also travelled to the Gulf States, and also, interestingly, Rwanda, Burundi and the Congo in search of low-skilled employment during the 1990s. There was also recruitment of Kenyan teachers to countries as diverse as the Comoros Islands, Seychelles, Rwanda, Burundi and the Congo.

In contrast, there are few accurate statistics about internal migration. Census material on migration is not available since the last published census in 1989, and there has been little analysis of this. It seems likely that areas around Nairobi and Mombasa and the coast, as well as areas of commercial farming, are net areas of immigration, whilst there continues to be net out-migration from much of Western and Northern Kenya.

Kenya also hosts refugees from the surrounding countries, and acts as a transit point for resettlement to third countries such as the US. In 2002, Kenya hosted just over 230,000 refugees and asylum seekers from neighbouring countries, notably Somalia and Sudan.[167] There are also significant numbers of IDPs in Kenya. The reasons for displacement are complex, but are linked to land redistribution, inter-ethnic clashes and the introduction of multi-party democracy in 1992. There are hopes that the NARC government under Mwai Kibaki elected in December 2002 will begin to solve some of the problems that caused these people to flee, and enable them to return home (see below).[168]

3.6.2 Importance of Migration to the Poor

The extent to which rural households engage in short- and long-term migration to maintain and diversify household income and reduce risk in the face of agro-climatic constraints is well documented in Kenya. Studies have shown that rural families increase their livelihood security by splitting the locations of the family, most often by one member of the family migrating to an urban area.[169] This may be necessary in marginal areas as there is insufficient economic capital in rural areas to diversify sources of income without migration.[170] Research carried out under the Natural Resources Policy Research Programme (NRPRP) shows in a small sample in Makueni district not only that over half of the households surveyed had access to migrant income, but that this was also larger and more secure than income from local wage labour, and had contributed to investment in farming.[171]

In addition to rural-urban migration, seasonal and temporary migration for agricultural employment is common in rural areas, and is used to increase family income. Pastoralists in northern Kenya still operate a nomadic or semi-nomadic lifestyle, with implications for access to services. In areas where families own marginal land the men will move seasonally to gain wage employment in order to provide cash to support their families which leads to short-term circulation patterns.[172]

However, most academic and policy attention has focused on rural-urban migration systems, which also commonly includes circulation. Agesa looks at the economic determinants of joint migration of the whole family against sequential migration of the (male) head of household, followed by the other members. He concludes that due to women's lower earning abilities in urban areas, families are likely to engage in sequential migration to decrease the costs and risks taken and to increase the benefits and income raised.[173] Higher levels of male education also contribute to greater levels of migration amongst men than amongst women.[174]

Path-breaking work in Western Kenya by John Hoddinott suggests that the decision to migrate, and remittance behaviour, are linked to a form of inter-

---

Box 11: The use of internal remittances in Kenya

The phenomenon of male labour migration from Western Kenya to urban areas has received considerable attention from economists. One study argues that through remittances and investment, this labour migration leads to a greater differentiation between the rich and poor farmers in the area, although most investment of remittances is not in land or farming techniques but on housing improvements and children's education.

Education also appears to be a major focus of the community, and remittances are often invested in school fees. Those who have educated relatives in urban areas also appear to receive larger remittances and are therefore able to send a higher proportion of their children to school, perpetuating inequality from one generation to the next.

Source: Francis (2002); see endnote 154.

generational 'migration contract' between a migrant and his or her parents, in which the (usually male) migrant moves and sends remittances in expectation of a subsequent inheritance.[175]

In terms of the consequences of migration for the poor, Oucho discusses the problems of balancing the costs and returns to rural areas of rural-urban migration, in terms of loss of labour, the cost of supporting the move, establishment in the town and returns in the forms of remittances, both economic and socio-cultural, and eventual return migration. He argues that migration creates dependency in rural areas of western Kenya on urban migrants and their remittances.[176]

In addition to internal migration, international migration also has consequences for the poor. Kenya is a country of origin and transit for trafficked persons, primarily women and children. Internal trafficking is reported to occur, with an estimated 200,000 street children in Kenya, a significant number of whom are believed to be engaged in forced labour or illegal activities, including prostitution.[177] Women are also reported to be trafficked to Lebanon and other Middle Eastern countries, while children are sent to Uganda. Women from Eastern Europe and Asia are also believed to be sent through Kenya en route to Western countries.

With respect to remittances from abroad, Kenya has no official data, but apparently received in the order of KSH 32 billion (about $420 million) in 2002.[178] Internal remittances are also significant, with recent estimates suggesting that migrants in urban areas remit between 13 and 22 per cent of their average incomes, whilst migration earnings constitute 20 per cent of total non-farm earnings even in remote rural areas, and up to 75 per cent of total non-farm earnings in areas close to major cities.[179]

In a recent study of how remittances are sent, the important role of commercial banks was highlighted. Services such as telegraphic transfers, electronic funds transfers and bank drafts are typically used for large value transfers, as they offer the cheapest service for the transfer of large amounts. However, for smaller amounts, informal means or post office transfers are used, the latter especially in the case of domestic transfers, while bus and courier companies were also noted as important means to transport remittances.[180]

3.6.3 International Migration and the Brain Drain

Evidence on the extent of the 'brain drain' in Kenya remains somewhat circumstantial, but this has not stopped the issue receiving some public prominence inside the country. Just 152 Kenyan trained nurses were registered to work in the UK in 2002/03, hardly a major problem if correct and reflected in other destination countries.[181] Yet it is reported that only one out of 14 recent recipients of doctoral degrees in molecular biology has stayed in the country to continue to conduct research, with the others moving to Europe or North America.[182]

Kenya's Health Minister, Charity Ngilu, is quoted as saying that out of 6,000 doctors trained in Kenya, just 600 remain in the country's public hospitals[183], whilst it is estimated that as many as 20 Kenyan doctors a month are leaving the country for better positions elsewhere.[184] A recent news article discussing why many professionals overseas do not want to return cited political instability as a major cause, as well as the lack of infrastructure.[185]

One point that should be borne in mind is that many people leave Kenya before they complete their university education, such that although they represent a 'brain drain' of sorts, the full cost of their education has not been met by the Kenyan state. It has been estimated that 30,000 Kenyans go overseas to study in Europe, the United States and Asia each year because of the limited access to higher education at home.[186]

3.6.4 Migration Policies

In general, policies that have been developed in Kenya in relation to migration view it rather negatively. Kenya's PRSP, although it is light on actual policy prescriptions, clearly has a negative view, stating that 'traditional systems (of social protection) are disappearing due to the breakdown of the extended family system, migration, economic hardships and poverty'.[187] Efforts have been made to stem the brain drain, although these have received press criticism, as some observers have accused the government of devaluing degrees and making them an expensive waste of time.[188] In particular, the introduction of parallel degree programmes, where students pay all of their fees themselves, has not overcome problems of quality control and quality assurance, whilst they appear to have created antipathy and resentment by students enrolled on state-funded degrees.

There have also been some attempts to reverse migration of the highly skilled. The MIDA scheme in Kenya run by IOM and its RQAN predecessor are reported to have returned over 300 professionals to Kenya by the end of 2002.[189] However, Okoth suggests that it is more important to encourage the diaspora to contribute to nation and economic building from outside the country, giving examples such as Africa Online, which was founded by a Kenyan in the US, rather than encouraging the highly skilled to return home in a situation where there are high levels of un- and underemployment.[190]

A recent and worrying development that runs somewhat counter to previous policy to reverse emigration is the decision by the government not to renew the visas of many expatriate workers where it is judged that a Kenyan could do the job as well.[191]

In relation to trafficking there are also problems, as the US State Department reports that Kenya does not fully comply with the minimum standards for the elimination of trafficking, even though it is making significant efforts to do so despite severe resource constraints[192] (e.g. the Children's Act of 2001 prohibits child labour that prevents children under 16 from going to school or that is exploitative and hazardous, and it also prohibits child sexual exploitation).

Community-based District Advisory Committees, set up to monitor child labour issues at district and local levels, have assisted 2,803 children, including 1,252 found working in hazardous conditions and 297 found working in forced labour conditions. The government is seeking to place street children in youth homes and social halls, providing them with meals and shelter to prevent them from being victimised. It also supports international organizations and NGOs to assist children in domestic service that includes education, skills training, counselling, legal advice, and a shelter for girls abused by their employers. A Human Trafficking Unit within the police was established in 2002, but its focus so far has been on immigration fraud. Government officials were implicated in identification fraud to facilitate illegal smuggling and six foreign nationals were deported for suspected smuggling of citizens to the Middle East.

One area in which there appears to be a gap in both knowledge and policy relates to the situation of those forcibly displaced within Kenya. International estimates put the number of IDPs in Kenya during the 1990s at over half a million, but despite the election of a new government in 2002, and a parliamentary commitment to resettle displaced people passed in July 2003, relatively few IDPs appear to have returned to their homes so far.[193]

A UN report on IDPs in Kenya noted that over 80 per cent of IDPs cited insecurity in their region of origin as their main reason for not returning.[194] Given that many IDPs are in urban areas and may be expected to remain there as part of ongoing urbanisation trends in the country, and the fact that resettlement proposals so far have been highly controversial, there is also a clear need for greater understanding of their situation and conditions in their current location.

3.7 Tanzania

3.7.1 Introduction

Like other countries in the region, there is a long history of rural-rural and rural-urban migration in Tanzania, dating to colonial and indeed pre-colonial times. The country also saw significant labour recruitment historically from neighbouring countries to provide a workforce for plantation agriculture. In post-independence Tanzania, following a socialist development path, long distance rural to rural migration slowed due to a policy focus on community level farming. However, seasonal labour migration still occurred in rural areas as extra labour was required during harvesting, e.g. to what were communal sisal farms near the coast.

Migration to urban areas has continued unabated, and increased during the programme of government decentralisation and the creation of new provincial capitals in the 1970s. Since the economic liberalisation in the 1980s, rural to urban migration has become more permanent, with migrants investing profits in ventures in or near the towns rather than remitting them to their areas of origin.

Tanzania has also seen a dramatic growth in its refugee population. At the height of the Great Lakes refugee crisis from 1993-98 nearly 1.3 million people arrived in western Tanzania as refugees from Rwanda and Burundi, an influx that increased the populations of the Kagera and Kigoma regions by more than 50 per cent.[195] At the end of 2002 there were still 689,000 refugees in the country, with around 57,000 returns, but also nearly 100,000 new arrivals during 2002.[196] These refugees were mainly from Burundi, but also included over 100,000 from the DRC. The vast majority of these refugees continue to be housed in Kagera and Kigoma, and fall under the responsibility of UNHCR.[197]

3.7.2 Importance of Migration to the Poor

Relatively good and recent information is available about the links between internal migration and poverty in Tanzania, thanks to an IIED study which looked at movement out of rural areas in both the North and South of the country.[198] In northern Tanzania, around Mt. Kilimanjaro, the migration of young people, both male and female, is very common as a way to increase opportunities, especially for marginalised women.[199]

In contrast to the situation in Kenya reported above, women were found more likely to migrate because daughters are usually excluded from land inheritance, so that they are encouraged to move away, either for marriage or work. Destinations of men and women were found to vary. Men were more likely to stay relatively close to their home area, or if they moved to Dar es Salaam, they were likely to be employed or apprenticed with a family member, whereas women were more likely to move further away, to Dar es Salaam or Mombasa, to reduce the shame to their families from working in bars or prostitution. These are often the only sources of employment open to women.

In southern Tanzania, in the remote area of Lindi, over 60 per cent of families interviewed were found to have at least one migrant family member, with this applying to households from across the economic spectrum.[200] Young single men were the biggest migrant group, and most went to Dar es Salaam to work as street vendors. Migrants did not move locally to Lindi town due to the lack of opportunities. Married men were more likely to engage in temporary rural agricultural migration on a seasonal basis. Some migrants also moved to settlements and were allocated access to land. Although migrants were found to maintain strong links with their rural origins, return migration remained very unusual. Remittance levels were found to have dropped in the last 10 years, due to increased costs of living.

Despite obvious difficulties faced by rural-urban migrants, it is interesting to note that they are not necessarily the poorest of city dwellers.[201] This may be partly because they work longer hours. However, where migrants find it difficult to survive in urban areas, this may lead them to invest their savings in the urban rather than rural areas. One survey from the early 1990s showed 90 per cent of urban migrants had bought land near to the town to farm, rather than investing in their home village, since this offered the chance to commute daily and was closer to urban produce markets.[202]

Recent work on remittances in Tanzania has found that intra-regional and domestic transfers remain costly as a result of limited money transfer options.[203] Whilst bank transfers are competitive for sending larger amounts in a single transaction, of much greater importance for the poor is the service offered by bus companies, which are making some inroads into a largely untapped market.[204] Informal means of transfer (e.g. sending money with relatives or returning with money to the home area) remain the most commonly used, especially for transfers of small amounts (but see also Box 12). It is worth noting that not just migrants, but also traders in rural areas, such as buyers of coffee, tea, tobacco, and other commodities, also tend to have to carry money to pay for the goods at the farm gate or trading centre where they purchase.

It is also important to pay attention to those in rural areas who are not receiving remittances, since they are likely to be the most vulnerable of all. One study of rural-urban migration has focused on the extreme poverty of women who are on their own through divorce or widowhood, who may be cut off from remittances previously provided by a partner, but unable to return to their natal home.

Clearly the presence of large numbers of refugees in Tanzania is also a matter of relevance to pro-poor policy. The coexistence of refugees and the host community in western Tanzania has been a major issue, since the livelihoods of refugees and host communities interact, in both positive and negative ways for the refugee and host populations.[205] Although many in the Tanzanian government have highlighted negative effects, it is worth noting that there are opportunities for local entrepreneurs to exploit the cheap labour and captive market that the camp dwellers provide. Refugees may benefit from local employment, which supplements income and food supplies, while increased local economic activity is good for both refugees and locals.

However, within the host communities there are others who do not benefit, either because they lack the social or economic capital to take advantage of the rapid influx of investment and business opportunities, or possibly because their own employment prospects are affected by refugees looking for work.

Tanzania is reported to be both a source and destination country for trafficked persons.[206] Children are reportedly trafficked internally from rural to urban areas for domestic work, commercial agriculture, fishing, mining, and prostitution, with refugee children perhaps especially vulnerable to being trafficked to work on Tanzanian farms. To a lesser degree, Tanzania is also reported to be a destination country for trafficked persons from India and Kenya.

Box 12: Changing attitudes to informal remittance transfer mechanisms

Despite noting the importance of informal remittance transfer mechanisms in East Africa in general, and especially for internal remittances, one important issue is that there appears to be growing mistrust in such informal transfer mechanisms, and growing demand for more formal money transfer mechanisms to be made available and accessible. Safety is a pervasive concern, and this is an area in which bus companies may fill an important niche.

Source: Sander (2003); see endnote 178.

3.7.3 Migration Policies

Policies on migration have been developed in several areas in Tanzania. First, as elsewhere in the continent, there has been some attempt to reduce rural-urban migration by focusing development initiatives on intermediate towns.[207] However, although this has given rise to some development, it has not reduced the levels of migration to large urban centres. More generally, there is little attempt in public policy-making to address the issue of voluntary or economic migration; the Tanzania PRSP fails to mention migration at all.

In relation to forced migration, meanwhile, a contrast can be drawn between policy on 'trafficking' and on refugees. In relation to 'trafficking', the US reports that Tanzania does not fully comply with minimum standards for the elimination of trafficking, although it is making significant efforts to do so.[208] There is a multi-agency government task force working on child labour, including public awareness campaigns, while a section of the penal code was enacted in 2001 that criminalises trafficking within or outside of Tanzania, although the penalty is seen as relatively light. During 2002, nightclubs were raided and 23 girls were repatriated to India for not having valid work permits. The owners were fined. However, financial constraints, corruption and a 'poor understanding of the scope of the problem' have contributed to a lack of government activity in this area.

In contrast, Tanzania's refugee policy was for many years hailed as a model of progressive legislation by refugee lawyers, even if some parallels can be found between the country's openness to refugees, and its historic recruitment of labour from neighbouring countries to work in the plantation sector. However, following the crises in Rwanda and Burundi in the mid-1990s, there has been a significant change of government policy.

The 1998 Refugee Act tightened the decision-making process to make it harder for asylum seekers to get refugee status, and reduced refugees' right to freedom of movement. After large-scale and largely forced repatriation of Rwandans in 1996, President Mkapa stated in May 2001 that all Burundian refugees should be repatriated, blaming the refugees for insecurity and the lack of development in western areas of Tanzania. Some repatriations to Burundi have occurred, although this continues to be problematic because of insecurity inside Burundi.[209]

As in other countries covered by this review, the significance of migration as a livelihood strategy remains a largely overlooked area for public policy in Tanzania. Although long abandoned as official government policy, the history of 'villagisation' programmes in the country arguably reinforced a mindset amongst policymakers that development was best promoted through interventions in rural areas that would reduce the need for migration. However, recent emphasis on decentralised development does recognise the need for rural people to have some level of mobility to smaller towns.

In addition, it is worth noting that Dar-es-Salaam has a longstanding reputation as a centre of learning for African professionals. Although this has declined somewhat in recent years in the face of economic decline, there is scope for Tanzania to promote mobility of professionals within the East African (or indeed sub-Saharan African) region, both to assist in the development of the city and its region, and to tackle the problem of 'brain drain' away from the continent.

3.8 Uganda

3.8.1 Introduction

In the late-colonial and early independence period, Uganda attracted labour migrants from neighbouring countries such as Rwanda and DRC to work on its plantations. However, with economic and political decline in the 1970s and 1980s, there was no longer any demand for immigrant labour and educated and professional Ugandans started to leave for neighbouring countries and the West, creating net out-migration. Since the late 1950s, Uganda has also received a large number of refugees from various crises and conflicts in the region, especially from DRC, Rwanda and Sudan.

There are no accurate figures on the number of Ugandans living outside Uganda: an anecdotal estimate suggests 500,000 emigrants, including refugees and migrants. At the end of 2002, there were around 38,000 Ugandan refugees registered worldwide, the majority in DRC.[210] UNDESA figures suggest net emigration of 14,000 each year from 1995-2000, with this figure predicted to rise in 2000-05.[211] Only small numbers appear as new entrants in Europe or the US, suggesting that most emigration is probably to other African countries such as Kenya, Tanzania, South Africa and Botswana.

In contrast, UNDESA figures suggest there were 529,000 immigrants in Uganda in 2000, representing 2.3 per cent of Uganda's population, although this is down from previous periods – it was estimated that in 1969, over 5 per cent of Uganda's total population were migrants, mostly other Africans.[212] At the end of 2002, just over 200,000 of these migrants were recognised refugees, although the real number of refugees and migrants is likely to be far greater. It is estimated that at least 50,000 refugees have self-settled and are not counted in these figures, while the Assistant Commissioner for Refugees has recently stated that Uganda hosts over 600,000 refugees alone, mainly from Sudan.[213]

This study has found no recent figures on internal labour migration in Uganda, although provisional data from the 2002 census is in the process of being published, and suggests that urbanisation has slowed considerably from 1991-2002. However, forced displacement has clearly increased in importance, with a report from September 2003 suggesting that the number of IDPs in Uganda had risen to over 1.4 million due to continued attacks in the North-West by the Lord's Resistance Army (LRA).[214] Since the 1990s, LRA attacks have caused periodic displacement of hundreds of thousands of people. The government has moved much of the population into 'protected villages', a controversial move which has unfortunately not been able to guarantee the protection of IDPs who suffer periodic attacks and daily violence.[215]

Another area of internal displacement has been the Rwenzori mountains in the west, as a result of attacks by the Allied Democratic Front (ADF), although security has now improved and people are returning. In eastern Uganda, thousands have been displaced by violent raids by Karamojong pastoralists.[216]

3.8.2 Importance of Migration to the Poor

Despite a lack of data on the movement of Ugandans either internally or abroad, it is striking that the most recent IMF figures for official remittances put the country in the top 20 countries worldwide in terms of the size of remittances proportional to GDP.[217] Thus, in 2001, the figure was estimated at $483 million, without counting informal remittances. This represents some 8.5 per cent of GDP, or nearly $20 per capita per annum, a sum that is higher than total foreign exchange earnings from coffee exports. An even higher figure of $600 million was quoted in a speech by the Minister of Internal Affairs of Uganda.[218] The local press has given a lot of attention to these figures in the recent past.

Some caution is needed with respect to these figures. First, the $483 million figure is composed of $283 million in private remittances and $128 million in NGO inflows, which are not obviously a result of migration. Second, these inflows were partly offset by private outflows of $190 million in the year, leaving net private remittances of just $94 million. Nonetheless, a recent study of remittance behaviour has also looked at how people transfer money, finding that informal transfers via friends and family were most common, especially as many formal mechanisms were geographically or financially inaccessible for many people. This would suggest that official remittance figures might still understate their total value.

A number of new, innovative mechanisms to transfer money are also worth highlighting. People wishing to send smaller amounts often use courier companies such as Elma Express and Yellow Pages, which have offices in most districts of Uganda. Users include internal migrants sending remittances and school fees to their families, and there is no limit on the amount that can be sent. A microfinance provider, Uganda Microfinance Union (UMU) has introduced a pilot money transfer product in one of its branches in 2001 and seems to have been successful in attracting clients, although currently these tend to be larger corporations and franchises as the fees remain high.

Remittances from migrants are clearly important for the poor, but they do not necessarily reach everyone. A recent study of livelihood strategies in Mbale, Kamuli and Mubende Districts compared female- and male-headed households, finding a greater number of economically active adults migrated from the former than the latter.[219] This affected male sons in particular. However, although remittances were found to play an essential role in female-headed households, this did not translate into enhanced income diversification, since off-farm opportunities for women were more circumscribed than for men.

There is also some evidence in Uganda of the association between HIV/AIDS and migration. Thus a longitudinal cohort study in a rural county of Masaka District found age and sex-standardised seroprevalence rates were 7.9 per cent overall, but only 5.5 per cent for adults who had not moved home; 8.2 per cent for adults who had moved within the village; 12.4 per cent for those who had moved to the neighbouring village; 11.5 per cent for those who had left the area; and 16.3 per cent for those who had joined the study area.[220] The reported number of lifetime sexual partners was higher for individuals who had changed residence.

A study on the livelihoods of self-settled urban refugees in Uganda suggests that despite some obstacles, many refugees possess skills, have been able to find employment and have either achieved self-sufficiency or are on the way to doing so.[221] The study therefore questions the policy of confining refugees to settlement camps where they cannot use their skills productively for themselves or the economy.

There are problems of internal and international trafficking (mainly to Sudan) of women and children, especially for labour and prostitution. In particular, the rebel group LRA has abducted tens of thousands of adults and children and forced them to become domestics, sex slaves or rebel soldiers.

3.8.3 International Migration and the Brain Drain

Uganda was one of the first countries in Africa to lose a significant proportion of its highly skilled population, mainly in response to economic and political decline in the 1970s and 1980s.[222] Education had expanded quickly in Uganda after independence and its schools and universities produced relatively highly-skilled people, who then could not find jobs. The main professionals leaving since the 1970s have been doctors, nurses, teachers/lecturers, engineers and scientists. Uganda was reported to have lost more than half its high-level and professional or technical personnel during Amin's rule from 1971-1979.

The first destinations were Kenya, Tanzania and South Africa, then Botswana and other African countries. A study from the 1980s found that Ghanaian and Ugandan nationals constituted 60 per cent of highly skilled migration into South Africa from East and West Africa at the time.[223] Another survey suggested net out-migration rates of up to 75,000 Ugandan nationals per year in the mid-1980s, of whom a high proportion were highly-skilled and professional migrants. An IMF study based on the 1990 US census shows 5,000 individuals born in Uganda living in the US, of whom nearly 4,000 were tertiary educated.[224] This was calculated to represent around 15 per cent of all those who had gained a tertiary education in Uganda.

One more recent study suggests that the exodus of skilled professionals has continued, although possibly at a lower rate. Thus an attempt to trace university graduates and secondary school leavers identified 414 graduates from four cohorts, of whom 321 were still in Uganda, 50 were deceased and 43 were overseas in late 2001.[225] This suggests a slightly lower level of international migration among graduates, although one in five graduates from 1980 was living outside Uganda in 2001, whilst of the 1999 graduates, 8 per cent were already living overseas in 2001. Male graduates were three times more likely to emigrate than female graduates.

The latter study is of particular interest, since it looks at cohorts of school leavers, and factors in where they obtained any higher education. Here, it is interesting to note a decline in higher education overseas, perhaps reflecting declining opportunities. Whereas 42 per cent of 1980 school leavers had gone on to higher education overseas, this figure had declined to 23 per cent in 1994 and just 13 per cent in 1999. However, the proportion of women going overseas for higher education had risen slightly over this period.

3.8.4 Migration Policies

In line with most other countries surveyed in this report, policy on migration in Uganda is broadly orientated towards international migration. Historically, this has involved measures to limit both emigration and immigration. In the late 1980s, Uganda instituted measures to restrict emigration of professionals and civil servants through the imposition of foreign exchange restrictions and obligatory clearance for travel abroad.[226] In 1990, the Government reported that it considered emigration levels to be too high and said it would take measures to reduce emigration. However, by 2000, the Government described emigration levels as 'satisfactory' and had moved to a policy of 'no intervention'.[227]

Uganda has participated in the Return of African Qualified Nationals Programme (RAQN), which has successfully returned Ugandans from the UK, India, Canada and US. Like other countries in SSA, it has more recently turned its attention to mobilising the diaspora without necessarily promoting return (e.g. government speakers have attended meetings of the Uganda North American Association to raise awareness of development objectives in Uganda).[228] A number of other Ugandan groups in the diaspora have also focused on development issues, such as a variety of Buganda organisations mainly in North America, but also in Sweden, and an Acholi organisation (Kacoke Madit) established by Acholi communities in the diaspora to promote conflict resolution initiatives in northern Uganda.[229]

Uganda has signed and ratified the 1951 Convention on Refugees and 1967 Protocol and ILO Convention 182 on Elimination of the Worst Forms of Child Labour. Uganda was also one of the first signatories of the International Convention on the Protection of the Rights of Migrant Workers and Members of their Families and acceded in 1995. It has not signed ILO Convention 97 on Migration for Employment, but it has launched a programme with the ILO to combat the worst forms of child labour as well as participated in the ILO regional programme to combat child labour in the commercial agricultural sector.

The legislative framework on child labour is quite weak and prosecution low, while overall, there remains limited institutional capacity on migration. Sections of the government involved in migration policy include the

Immigration Department in the Ministry of Internal Affairs (immigration 'facilitation', monitoring and control), The Population Secretariat in the Ministry of Finance, Planning and Economic Planning (population policy, programmes and research), and the Uganda Bureau of Statistics (national migration statistics). The 1995 Constitution also stipulates the establishment of a National Citizenship and Immigration Board, although no evidence of its existence or work was found. In addition, Makerere University hosts the Refugee Law Project and other institutions do limited work on migration, such as the Centre for Basic Research and the Makerere Institute for Social Research.

Uganda's refugee policy is still guided by the outdated 1960 Control of Aliens Act, which has been criticised for its inconsistency with international refugee law especially as regards the rights of refugees to own property, have access to courts and enjoy freedom of movement. Uganda has been discussing a new refugee law for some years and in December 2003, it was approved by the Cabinet and passed to Parliament. Meanwhile, the government has been implementing a Self-Reliance Strategy (SRS) programme to try to promote integration of refugee assistance and local development, although this has also been criticised for concentrating almost entirely on the integration of service provision and not wider economic and social integration.

The protection of refugees and especially IDPs in Uganda is a pressing problem. Every month there are abductions and killings in IDP camps in the northwest and the government's policy of grouping the population in camps does not seem to be offering any protection. On occasion the government has been accused of forcibly removing refugees from Uganda.

The Uganda PRSP (or PEAP) does not mention migration or refugee issues, nor do the 2001 and 2002 APRs. However, the 2003 APR does mention the issue of refugees in Uganda, commenting on the high numbers of poor rural refugees and their impacts on the social and economic development of local/host populations.[230] These are mainly expressed in negative terms such as potential environmental damage (depletion, degradation of natural resources, scarcity of water), stretching of social amenities and food shortages.

However, the APR also mentions possible positive effects of refugee presence including that international assistance to refugees may bring new services and infrastructure if properly planned and thus help development of the host region. The presence of refugees may also spark economic development if it brings additional market outlets, economic opportunities and innovative skills and practices.

The APR also discusses the draft Refugee Bill to be tabled to Cabinet and

Parliament in 2003. This aims to integrate refugee services within district development plans recognising that refugees and local communities share services. Thus Self Reliance Strategies (SRS) will be introduced for this purpose to avoid the establishment of parallel structures and 'foster the capacity of refugees to sustain themselves by allowing them to cultivate land, grow crops and to generate food and income in order to make them self-reliant'.

In contrast to the PRSP, Uganda's latest Participatory Poverty Assessment (PPA) in 2000 does have a short discussion of migration as an economic or coping strategy. Noting that people migrate because of insecurity, to search for livelihood opportunities or seasonal water for animals, or to seek better services, it suggests that migrants find life hard but may succeed. Migrant men are described as often living in sub-standard accommodation and eating modestly, but being respected in their communities of origin where they are seen as better off. In addition to migration from all districts to Kampala, rural-rural migration is also noted from Kalangala, Kapchorwa, Kisoro, Kabarole and Bushenyi districts.

Box 13: Turnaround of policy on emigration

The extent of the turnaround in policy on emigration from Uganda is quite substantial, and according to recent articles in the New Vision and Monitor newspapers, reflects the new goal of the Ugandan Government to develop the potential economic contribution of the diaspora, rather than encouraging them not to leave.

For example, the liberalisation of financial markets, especially trade in foreign exchange, and the granting of permission for foreign denominated bank accounts, are said to have increased remittances. The Bank of Uganda Forex and Trade Department is now generally supportive and positively inclined towards granting permission to Money Transfer Organisations (MTOs).

There is also some interest in using Micro-Finance Institutions (MFIs) as providers of money transfer services. For example, the Centenary Rural Development Bank, a microfinance bank, represents one of the global MTOs, Western Union, as a sub-agent to a commercial bank, Nile Bank. An interviewee in DFID Kampala suggested the government now actually supports people going abroad to gain experience and has been engaged in training in this respect.

Source: DFID Uganda

Although remittances are seen as playing an important part in rural people's lives, with receipt of cash from children in the city as an important means of survival for many elderly people, they are also described as a 'vulnerable source of income'. Migration of relatives to Kampala is seen as placing an initial strain on household resources.

At present, the Ugandan government's capacity on migration issues seems to be almost wholly focused on immigration controls and statistics. There is a need to engage in capacity building so that the government can also examine migration and development issues and develop strategies. In particular, there is very little hard data or knowledge on the levels, nature and implications of internal migration in Uganda and the links between migration and livelihoods. The lack of reliable estimates of the numbers, location and status of Ugandans abroad may also be an impediment to programmes to engage the diaspora in Uganda's development. There is also a particular need to collect more information on self-settled refugees.

There is particular potential to build on new mechanisms for money transfer in Uganda such as courier companies and microfinance institutions to increase the possibilities of safe, cost-effective money transfer for internal and international migrants. More research on the links between migration and development might also help the government to develop a better understanding of the importance and risks of migration for the poor and develop strategies that can be integrated into the PRSP and rural development plans.

In addition:

- Further research on brain drain could also be done to get more accurate figures and details of the professions and destinations of those leaving. Uganda could learn from other countries that have put in place policies on brain drain, such as enhancing training and facilitating return.

- Uganda still hosts significant numbers of refugees and needs continuing support in this respect. In particular, there are a large number of self-settled refugees about whom less is known. The Refugee Law Project at Makerere University has been working with this latter group and its research could be used to better inform policy.

- The levels of internal displacement and attacks on IDPs have now reached very high levels and there is an urgent need to find solutions to the conflict situation in the region and in the meantime to investigate better protection measures for IDPs.

- Finally, there is a need for more research and understanding of the problems of trafficking and exploitation of women and children in Uganda and a more comprehensive government strategy, which prioritises protection and rights. There is also a need for Uganda to develop specific anti-trafficking legislation.

3.9 Rwanda

3.9.1 Introduction

There has been significant movement within, from and to Rwanda over past decades, especially forced migration due to conflict and famine. Labour migration, notably to the mines of DRC and plantations of Uganda, was important in the colonial and post-colonial period. Due to the complexities and scale of these historical population movements and a lack of statistics, it is difficult to obtain accurate figures on the current numbers of Rwandan nationals living outside Rwanda.

A recent website established by the Rwandan government estimates that there are more than 100,000 economically productive Rwandans outside the country, but this is widely thought to be an underestimate.[231] Rwanda Information Exchange has previously given a figure of 300,000 and in an interview with the Director of Immigration of the Government, he suggested the figure could be as high as 600,000.[232]

As is the case with all such migration statistics, the problem is compounded by problems over whom to count. There are officially registered refugees and migrants, unregistered and self-settled refugees and migrants, asylum seekers, the children of Rwandan refugees or migrants born elsewhere, as well as those who are naturalised but consider themselves Rwandan and still maintain links. One author estimates that there were 3.7 million people of Rwandan origin living in neighbouring countries – principally Zaire – in 1990, over and above official refugee figures.[233]

UNDESA figures show huge inflows and outflows for Rwanda over the last decade, but this reflects the war, genocide and mass returns from 1994-98, and tells us little about underlying population movements.[234] In contrast, Eurostat figures show that an average of just 694 Rwandan immigrants entered the EU each year from 1995-2001. According to UNHCR, there were 75,000 Rwandan refugees and asylum seekers worldwide at the end of 2002, the majority in African countries – especially DRC and Uganda – with about 10,000 Rwandan refugees in OECD countries.

In terms of inflows, UNDESA figures gave a migrant stock of 89,000 in 2000, representing 1.2 per cent of Rwanda's population.[235] At the end of 2002, there were just under 35,000 refugees, almost all from the DRC.[236] Unlike most neighbouring countries, internal migration rates appear to be low. Household surveys in 2000-01 revealed only 9 per cent of the population were living outside their province of birth (684,000 people). Kigali is the main destination, accounting for 37 per cent of internal migration.[237]

Rwanda has not only produced large numbers of refugees, but also up to 650,000 IDPs at the peak of internal displacement in 1998.[238] Officially there are no longer any IDPs in Rwanda as they have been resettled. However, in October 2001, a multi-agency mission including UN, donor and Rwandan government representatives found there were still some 192,000 people living in IDP-like conditions, and it seems unlikely that this number has since decreased.

There are also problems of internal and international trafficking of women and children, especially for labour and prostitution.[239] There are an estimated 2,000 child prostitutes in Rwanda, and tens of thousands of street children exploited for labour, plus some abductions by rebel militia. The government has been recently criticised for forcible round-ups of street children and their internment in centres where they are fed and receive training, but have no liberty.

Box 14: IDPs and villagisation in Rwanda

Estimates of the number of IDPs in Rwanda are controversial partly due to the Rwandan government's National Habitat Policy of villagisation (imidugudu). This policy was launched in 1996, both to solve acute housing needs of returnees and as a rural development strategy. However, from 1996-2000, there was some evidence of forcible movement of people into such planned villages.

Accusations of forced movement to planned villages have subsided since 2000, but the policy of villagisation remains and there are questions about whether this programme will be forced or voluntary in the future. Furthermore, the key element of Rwanda's draft land policy is land consolidation. If this is implemented, it may result in a far larger landless class, demand for labour on small plantations and an increase in internal migration.

3.9.2 Importance of Migration to the Poor

Compared with other African countries, rates of internal migration in Rwanda are low. This is related to the nature of Rwanda's geography and rural economy, but also to past political controls on internal movement, which made it difficult for people to move especially in the 1980s and early 1990s. Although there is no policy of control in place at present, there are still some reports of the authorities creating obstacles to movement and of problems in receiving communities.

Reflecting this lack of internal movement, there are virtually no studies in Rwanda of the links between migration, poverty and livelihoods, the importance of remittances, or their intergenerational impacts. Anecdotal evidence from NGOs suggests the causes of migration include periodic or chronic food insecurity; land pressure due to population density and continuous division of household land; and the chance of better employment, education and training opportunities. There is also some evidence from food security surveys of significant periodic and seasonal movement due to periodic or chronic food insecurity.[240]

Chronic food insecurity in a N-S band west of Kigali (especially parts of Gikongoro, Butare and Gitarama) appears to have caused migration eastwards, and to provincial towns. At the present time, failed crops in Kigali-Ngali and parts of Kibungo have also caused fairly significant movement to Umutara and Kigali, whilst there are likely to be some migrant labourers working in the tea plantations of Butare and Gikongoro. There also appears to be a recent growth in rural-urban migration, focused almost entirely on Kigali. Urbanisation remains low in Rwanda at around 10 per cent, but the government's 2020 Vision Strategy anticipates that this will rise to 30 per cent by 2020.[241]

IMF figures on international remittances are also sketchy and incomplete, suggesting just $31 million between 1990-99, or just one per cent of all resource flows to the country. The Rwandan Ministry of Finance has, however, reported a figure of $40 million in official remittances for 2001 alone, and admits this is likely to be a significant underestimate.

3.9.3 International Migration and the Brain Drain

The limited figures that exist suggest that levels of emigration of tertiary educated and professionals are also currently relatively low for Rwanda.[242] This may reflect the relatively low past level of tertiary level training in Rwanda, although now the government is promoting higher education especially in sectors such as ICTs, business administration and management, rates of emigration may increase.

However, as noted above, there may be quite a substantial Rwandan diaspora, which certainly includes a large number of the intelligentsia and professional classes under the old regime. One relevant factor is that this group is very politically active. There are a number of opposition parties and platforms based in Europe and North America including INHANGO and CPODR (Concertation Permanente de l'Opposition Democratique Rwandaise) and the head of the banned MDR party, Faustin Twagiramungu, remains in exile in Belgium. In the absence of strong opposition inside Rwanda, these exiled opposition parties in some ways represent an alternative political voice (not all are extremists). Some have a large following amongst the diaspora, but it is not clear what support they enjoy amongst the population inside Rwanda.

3.9.4 Migration Policies

The parts of the Rwandan government involved in migration issues and policy include:

- General Direction for Immigration and Emigration in the National Security Office: focus is currently on immigration controls, although there are plans to make it into a Migration Department with a mandate to oversee migration policy and strategy.

- Ministry of Foreign Affairs: oversees issues to do with Rwandan refugees and migrants overseas and has a new diaspora and development desk; looks after the Rwandan Global Diaspora Network.

- Ministry of Finance and Economic Planning: oversees remittance issues

- Ministry of Education: nominal brief on brain drain.

- National Statistics Office: monitors national migration statistics, but for now limited to census results.

- National Refugee Council: established to oversee asylum cases and draw up a new immigration and asylum law.

In 2001, the government launched the Rwanda Global Diaspora Network (RGDN). One of the aims of this network is to establish a Diaspora Investment Bank, to try to promote the productive investments and savings of the diaspora.

The launch took place at the First Rwandan Diaspora Global Convention, held in Kigali in December 2001. There were 385 representatives from the Rwanda diaspora in 32 countries. Although this is an excellent initiative, it should be noted that reporting on other Rwandan websites at the time (not pro-government) were critical and said that those members of the diaspora who went were hand-picked and the government failed to attract many Hutus.

In relation to emigration, the Director for Immigration and Emigration reports that nothing is done to stop movement abroad, except that the Ministry of Education (MINEDUC) has recently changed its policy on overseas scholarships to try to encourage students to return to Rwanda afterwards. There are some initiatives to promote return of Rwandans from abroad. As well as the UNHCR voluntary return agreements, one aim of the RGDN is to engage diaspora skills and knowledge to contribute to Rwanda's development. Rwanda has held discussions with IOM about a possible return scheme, and also with UNDP, which is launching a TOKTEN programme that aims to bring back short-term volunteers in engineering, medicine, and education. This will

Box 15: Regional migration arrangements

A question for the future is whether or not Rwanda will join the East Africa Community (EAC) with Tanzania, Uganda and Kenya and thus, whether or not the proposed provisions on free movement of skilled or all labour will become a reality. Rwanda applied a few years ago and its application was refused the first time. However, the application is still on the table and the EAC has promised to consider the issue of new members later this year once the EAC customs union is operational after March.

In the past, Rwanda was part of CEPGL (Communité Economique des Pays des Grands Lacs), which was established in 1976 by Rwanda, Zaire and Burundi. In 1985 CEPGL adopted a convention on the free movement of persons, goods and services, capital and rights of establishment in member countries. However, low prevailing skill levels kept movement of high-level personnel among these countries to a minimum (unlike Uganda with its good quality higher education, Rwanda and Burundi have tended to rely on institutions in the US, Europe and Russia for university education) and these protocols were never properly translated into national legislation. Furthermore, since the 1990s, conflict in the Great Lakes region led to the breakdown of CEPGL. At present there is little likelihood that it will be revived in the near future.

focus on attracting qualified expatriate nationals as short-term volunteers, and the US$5 million project has been designed with MINEDUC (Ministry of Education) and the Human Resource Development Agency (HRDA). Rwanda has signed and ratified the 1951 Convention on Refugees and 1967 Protocol and ILO Convention 182 on Elimination of the Worst Forms of Child Labour. It has also recently signed Protocols of the UN Convention against Transnational Organised Crime including on Trafficking. It has not signed the International Convention on the Protection of the Rights of Migrant Workers and Members of their Families.

Rwanda does not currently have an immigration and asylum policy. In the aftermath of the genocide, UNHCR handled these issues, but in 2001 Rwanda set up a National Refugee Council to rule on claims on a case-by-case basis and to develop a new immigration and asylum law. The draft law should go to Parliament this year.

Overall, Rwanda does not currently have explicit migration policies or activities in other areas such as migrant protection or trafficking, nor is there currently huge press attention to the issue. The PRSP makes a passing mention to the reintegration challenges since 1994 but does not specifically mention migration, whilst the PPA makes no mention of migration issues at all. The Rwandan media gives regular coverage to refugee issues, especially about returning refugees and the government's refugee repatriation programme, but otherwise, there are hardly any reports about migration, aside from occasional reporting about migrants from neighbouring countries who live and work illegally in Rwanda. Finally, Vision 2020 sets out some of the broad lines of the strategies of villagisation, land consolidation, urbanisation and decentralisation.

The Rwandan government has faced many challenges since 1994 and developing policies and strategies on migration issues has clearly not been a major priority. However, it does now appear to recognise that it needs to look at these issues and develop clear strategies.

A first priority appears to be the finalisation of the immigration and asylum law in accordance with international standards. Research is needed on the links between migration and development such that migration issues can be integrated into the PRSP and rural development strategies as necessary. There is some concern within government about the current concentration of rural-urban migration on Kigali and policy is seeking to focus some urbanisation of the other 12 main municipalities.

A number of other areas can be highlighted where further work would be helpful:

- It would be useful to understand whether there are de facto bureaucratic controls on population movement, whilst research on remittances in Rwanda – internal and international – including on the levels of formal and informal remittances, remittance behaviour and possible schemes to promote productive use of remittances would also be of value.

- Although brain drain does not currently seem to be a problem, it may become an issue in the future and the government could usefully learn from the experiences of other countries in putting in place policies to enhance the positive effects and minimise the negative effects of educated and professionals leaving.

- Programmes should be encouraged and supported to engage the diaspora productively and also increase confidence about long-term return, whilst an attempt should be made to better understand the transnational activities of the diaspora and their impacts in Rwanda.

- Underpinning some of the existing policy gaps is the lack of reliable estimates of the numbers, location and status of Rwandans abroad, and of the scale and nature of internal movements. Indeed, given the massive inflows and outflows due to the conflict and genocide, and the lack of statistics, it is hard to get an idea of the levels of voluntary or labour migration of Rwandans, whether internally or internationally. The government is aware that this is an important issue and would like to commission some research in this area.

- Rwanda needs to develop its capacity to collect and monitor both international and internal migration statistics with the cooperation of destination countries. There is a need to continue to monitor the flow of asylum seekers out of Rwanda even if the numbers are limited. The majority of the political opposition is in exile and some of those who continue to leave cite the tight political control and inability to criticise the government. Refugee flows and returns may be a good barometer of the political environment.

- There is also a need to monitor the situation of Rwandan refugees to ensure they are being accorded adequate protection in their countries of asylum and that return programmes are voluntary. The case of the thousands of unregistered or self-settled refugees in Uganda and DRC is particularly challenging as these refugees lack status and protection.

- The future implementation of Rwanda's Habitat and Land policies is intended to promote the movement of the population to villages and cities and the consolidation of agricultural land. This will need monitoring closely to ensure movements are voluntary. Also, if implemented these policies may well provoke an increase in internal migration.

- Finally, there is a need for more research and understanding of the problems of trafficking and exploitation of women and children in Rwanda and a more comprehensive government strategy which prioritises protection and rights.

MIGRATION & DEVELOPMENT IN SOUTHERN AFRICA

4.1 Overview

- Southern Africa has a long history of intra-regional labour migration, dating back to the mid-nineteenth century. Migration was the single most important factor underlying the emergence of a single regional labour market. Longstanding patterns, forms, and dynamics of migration have undergone major restructuring in the last two decades with considerable implications for sound migration management, livelihood strategies of the poor, human rights observance, and poverty and inequality reduction policies.

- The end of apartheid, the integration of South Africa with the SADC region and SADC's reconnection with the global economy have brought a major increase in legal and undocumented cross-border flows and new forms of intra-regional mobility.

- Growing rural and urban poverty and unemployment have pushed more people out of households in search of a livelihood. One aspect of this has been the feminization of poverty in rural Southern Africa and a significant gender reconfiguration of migration streams.

- Southern Africa has experienced a major depletion of its human resource base through emigration ('brain drain') over the last two decades. South Africa and Zimbabwe are most affected. No countries have developed successful retention strategies or offsetting immigration strategies.

- Migration is a critically important survival strategy for hundreds of thousands of households throughout the region. This reality is rarely recognised in policies directed at poverty and inequality reduction.

- Recurrent civil strife in the rest of Africa has generated mass refugee movements and new kinds of asylum seekers to and within the region. The cessation of hostilities and threat has confronted countries of asylum with issues of repatriation and integration.

- Supporting regional integration and cooperation within Southern Africa is a major goal of SADC, and is also consistent with NEPAD. Migration is a major cross-cutting issue in the recent SADC Regional Indicative Strategic Development Plan.

- Regional policy forums such as the Migration Dialogue for Southern Africa (MIDSA) represent an important vehicle for promoting regional inter-state dialogue, migration policy harmonization and raising the national and regional profile of migration as a development issue.

- Development projects and programmes specifically targeted at mobile populations have not been a major feature. Migrants are the incidental beneficiaries or victims of other interventions (e.g. rural development, trade policy, food security programmes). Mainstreaming migration means foregrounding migrant populations and communities as viable agents of self-development.

- Migration data collection and analysis is outdated and unusable to policy-makers in many countries. Initiatives to build a local sustainable capacity for migration information collection and analysis (within and outside government as appropriate) could be supported.

- The extent to which rural and urban households engage in internal and cross-border migration to maintain incomes and reduce risk has been seriously underestimated in Southern Africa. The failure of governments and international agencies to integrate migration impacts into poverty and inequality reduction strategies is one unfortunate consequence. Not only is better information needed on the poverty reduction potential of migration, but concrete strategies need to be developed to assist migrants and migrant households to maximise the benefits of migration (e.g. through support of migrant and refugee associations, burial societies, micro-credit facilitation, rural cooperatives, and migrant SMMEs).

- The relationship between migration and HIV/AIDS is increasingly clear. Migration is a vector for disease transmission, but mobile populations are particularly vulnerable to infection. A review of past experiences and programmes would assist the development of appropriate models of prevention, peer education, palliative care and treatment roll-out plans. At the regional level, the development of the Partnership for HIV/AIDS And Mobile Populations in Southern Africa (PHAMSA) is an important new research, policy, advocacy and networking possibility deserving of support. Finally, there is a significant dearth of capacity in the management and evaluation of HIV/AIDS project programming, leading to poor implementation and results. Training initiatives to build capacity could enhance outcomes associated with improved management of the epidemic. Existing programmes directed at migrants and migrant populations are not working. A sounder knowledge base would assist in the development of workable models.

- As regards policy reform, several countries in the region have recently overhauled or are in the process of reforming outdated immigration and migration laws. The quest for greater control underpins these initiatives. Migration policy and legislation needs to be read and reformed in ways that facilitate economic development and alleviate poverty. The development and implementation of new policy needs to be given a pro-poor optic to assess the implications for the poor. Where these consequences are negative or non-facilitative, these need to be brought to the attention of policymakers and adjustments sought. At the regional level, SADC and COMESA have both developed plans for greater freedom of movement along the EU model. Individual countries have been wary of, and stymied, this process. A systematic regional study of the positive and negative implications of freedom of movement is long overdue.

- The amount of basic information on migration causes, consequences and impacts has grown considerably in recent years. South Africa is particularly well-researched in this regard, other countries less so. A long-term governmental capacity for collecting nationally representative migration information at the household level needs to be developed. National migration household surveys conducted at regular intervals would provide invaluable data on migration/poverty connections and allow monitoring of change over time. National statistical offices, working in regionally coordinated fashion, would be the best location for such a venture.

- The lack of reliable data on the numbers and transnational connections of Southern Africans living abroad is an obvious gap. The potential of diasporic connections in facilitating development has not been addressed.

- Regional economic integration and harmonization of migration and immigration policies is a matter of urgency for the Southern African region. The likely impact of greater freedom of movement within SADC is unknown. A systematic study of this issue would help countries make a realistic assessment of consequences.

4.2 Region-Wide Issues

Migration was probably the single most important factor tying together all of the various colonies and countries of the sub-continent into a single regional labour market during the twentieth century.

Established patterns, forms, and dynamics of migration have undergone major change in the last two decades with considerable implications for livelihood strategies of the poor and for government poverty and inequality reduction policies. Southern Africa is now, quite literally, a region on the move.[243] Several fundamental reasons are responsible for this dynamic state of affairs:

- The end of apartheid, a system designed to control movement and exclude outsiders at all costs, produced new opportunities for internal and cross-border mobility and new incentives for moving.

- The ensuing integration of South Africa with the SADC region brought new forms of intra-regional mobility.

- More broadly, South Africa's reconnection with the global economy has opened the country and region up to forms of migration commonly associated with globalization.[244]

- Domestically, rural and urban poverty have pushed more people to move in search of a livelihood. The feminization of poverty in rural Southern Africa and a significant gender reconfiguration of migration streams have resulted.[245]

- HIV/AIDS has also impacted considerably on migration. Not only is the rapid diffusion of the epidemic itself inexplicable without reference to the mobility of people but new forms of migration are emerging in response.[246]

- Finally, the social and economic impact of the Mozambican and Angolan civil wars continue to reverberate. Recurrent civil strife in the rest of Africa has generated mass refugee movements and new kinds of asylum seekers to and within the region. The cessation of hostilities and threat has confronted countries of asylum with issues of repatriation and integration.

Regional and national programmes and migration policy responses directed at poverty and inequality reduction within migrant communities and between migrants and non-migrants must take cognizance of the extraordinary dynamism and instability of migration forms and patterns in the region. Governments wedded to legal frameworks of control and exclusion are finding it increasingly difficult to cope. The fundamental policy challenge is to move the states of Southern Africa to a regionally harmonised and consistent set of policies that emphasise good governance, sound management and client-centred service delivery.[247] In addition, because migration is a cross-cutting phenomenon, it needs to be integrated into all facets of state policymaking and planning, including programmes and strategies to alleviate poverty and reduce inequality. For this to happen, migration's key role needs to be documented by researchers and recognised by policymakers.

This section highlights the continuities and changes in the regional migration regime over the last two decades. Subsequent sections examine the policy implications of these changes. The states of Southern Africa can be divided into migrant-sending (Mozambique, Malawi, Lesotho) and migrant-receiving states (Botswana, Namibia). A few, such as South Africa, fall into both categories. Others, such as Tanzania and Zambia, have experienced major refugee influxes in the last decade but do not tend to send or receive large numbers of labour migrants. Several migration streams can be identified. Trends increasingly evident in each category can be expected to continue in the foreseeable future:

- Restructuring of traditional contract labour systems

- Growth in the volume and complexity of cross-border mobility

- Declining levels of legal migration to and within the region

- Expansion in undocumented migration and human trafficking

- Increase in skills brain drain from the region

- Resettlement and reintegration of mass refugee movements

- Feminization of cross-border migration

- Growth in intra-regional, informal, cross-border trade

- Rapid urbanization and reconfiguration of rural-urban linkages

Male labour migration to the mines (of South Africa, Zambia, Zimbabwe) and commercial farms and plantations (South Africa, Zimbabwe, Swaziland) is the most enduring form of legal cross-border labour migration within the region, beginning in the late nineteenth century and continuing to the present.[248] Mine migration was the most highly regulated through systems of recruitment under a single agency, the Employment Bureau of Africa (TEBA).

By the 1990s only the South African gold and platinum mines continued to employ large numbers of domestic and foreign migrants; other mining sectors in South Africa (such as coal mining) and elsewhere in the region (Zambia, Zimbabwe) had moved to local and/or stabilised workforces before the 1990s.[249] During the 1990s, the South African mines experienced major downsizing and retrenchments creating considerable social disruption and increased poverty in supplier areas. Interestingly, the mines laid off local workers at a much faster rate than foreign workers. As a result, the proportion of foreign workers rose from 40 per cent in the late 1980s to close to 60 per cent today. This 'externalization' of the workforce was particularly beneficial to Mozambique. Mozambicans now make up 25 per cent of the mine workforce, up from 10 per cent a decade ago.

Remittance levels have remained stable in Mozambique but fell during the 1990s to many areas, especially Lesotho, Swaziland and the Eastern Cape. This has presented a major challenge for households formerly reliant on mine remittances. Poverty levels have increased as have domestic and family tensions. Other family members have begun to migrate in response. Various efforts have been made to soften the impacts of retrenchments. These include the community development programmes of the Mineworkers Development Agency, the CARE programme adopted by Canadian-owned Placer Dome, the rural development programmes of TEBA and an IOM project on retrenched miners.[250] The overall impact of these interventions has yet to be systematically assessed but initial signs are not that encouraging.

The numbers of people legally crossing borders throughout the Southern African region has exploded in the last decade. In South Africa, for example, the annual number of legal visitors from other SADC countries has increased from around 1 million in the early 1990s to over 5 million at the present time. Border posts throughout the region have experienced major increases in the volume of human traffic. The pressure on limited border control resources has been enormous, with long delays and inefficiency experienced at many border posts. Corruption has become endemic at many posts as travellers seek to jump queues and gain unlawful entry. In addition, the region has experienced a major influx of Africans from other parts of the country as well as significant growth in tourism arrivals from overseas. Intra-regional tourism has also grown to significant levels.

South African stated-purpose-of-entry data is available by country from Statistics South Africa on a monthly basis. Although limited to designated categories (holiday, business, study, work, immigration), the numbers do not suggest that the majority of people enter for work or work-seeking. This is confirmed by SAMP research which reveals a multiplicity of motives for cross-border movement.[251] Cumulatively, in 6 SADC countries less than 25 per cent of international migrants moved to work or look for work. However, there was considerable inter-country variation: Mozambique (67 per cent), Zimbabwe (29 per cent), Lesotho (25 per cent), Namibia (13 per cent) and Swaziland (9 per cent). Other major reasons included visiting/tourism: Namibia and Swaziland (58 per cent), Lesotho (36 per cent), Mozambique (17 per cent), and Zimbabwe (16 per cent); and trading and shopping: Zimbabwe (42 per cent), Lesotho (22 per cent); Swaziland (12 per cent), Mozambique (6 per cent), and Namibia (3 per cent). Relatively minor reasons included study, business, and medical treatment. Available data from other SADC countries shows a marked increase in inward and outward legal border crossing in most other states.[252] Studies also show similar variety in stated reasons for entry. Again, the primary stated reason is not to work but for visiting, tourism and trade and business.

SAMP research shows that the majority of cross-border migrants in Southern Africa remain circular migrants. In other words, although many stay for longer than initially intended their visits are generally seen as temporary not permanent. Across a whole range of indices, migrants tend to prefer living in their own countries. The major migrant-receiving countries (South Africa, Botswana) are seen as superior only in terms of employment and economic opportunity and perhaps health facilities. In every other respect – personal and family safety, educational opportunities, access to land, national culture, etc. – home countries are viewed as preferable. The obvious conclusion is that economic stability and growth at home is the single most important factor in slowing labour migration across borders. The only major exception to the tendency of impermanence is in the case of Mozambicans who came to South Africa during the civil war of the 1980s and have stayed rather than return.

Most countries of the region tend to see in-migration more as a threat than an opportunity. Migrants are viewed as carriers of disease, takers of jobs and perpetrators of crime. Policy has tended to focus, as a result, on control and exclusion. Unfortunately, this general mentality extends to legal immigration. Few, if any, of the SADC states have pro-active immigration policies. Rights of permanent residence and settlement are extremely difficult to obtain in most countries. Until the 1990s, South Africa was the only country with a pro-active immigration policy (in that case to recruit white immigrants to boost the economy and shore up white rule). After 1994, even South Africa became an anti-immigrationist state. After independence, most countries did solicit foreign skilled workers on contract in the public sector but this was always subject to active Africanization and localization employment policies. Only Botswana has taken a more open position on skilled immigration, but there are strong indications that this too is about to change.

Clearly, pervasive anti-immigrationist policies are at odds with the realities of globalization and global skills markets. SADC is in significant danger of becoming a seller but never a buyer in this marketplace, to its own detriment. Events such as the decimation of workforces by HIV/AIDS may force the region's hand, but for now it appears that most countries are more prepared to rail against and try and prevent the exodus of skilled nationals than adopt pro-active immigration policies to attract economic immigrants from other jurisdictions in order to stimulate growth and employment.

The migrant stream that attracts most public and official attention is 'undocumented' or 'illegal' or 'unauthorised' migration. The first point to emphasise is that clandestine border crossing in Southern Africa is nothing new. Second, while the volume has undoubtedly increased in the last two decades, it hardly warrants the aquatic imagery that is generally applied to the phenomenon ('floods', 'tidal waves', etc.). Third, undocumented migration tends to be driven by economic circumstances and, in some cases, desperation. Finally, enforcement in all countries tends to focus on identifying and deporting violators with the minimum of due process. In terms of sheer volume, South Africa is easily the regional leader, having deported over one million people since 1990. Significantly, the vast majority of deportees (upwards of 80 per cent) are sent home to only two countries, Mozambique and Zimbabwe. Tensions between these countries have simmered below the surface on this issue for some time. Bilateral commissions have done little to either stop the flow of migrants or change the mentality of exclusion and control.

Studies of sectors where undocumented migrants are employed in the region have revealed consistent violation of labour standards, sub-minimum wages, rampant economic and sexual exploitation, and great instability and fear among migrants. These sectors include commercial agriculture, construction and secondary industry.[253] A systematic regional investigation of undocumented migration and irregular employment has yet to be undertaken.[254]

The fundamental contradiction facing most countries is this: enhanced regional integration would suggest the need for greater mobility in the factors of production (including labour) but nationalist sentiments cast foreigners as a threat to the job security of citizens. As long as migration is viewed as a threat not an opportunity for sending and receiving states, the legal drawbridge is likely to remain up. Without legal means to sell their labour or pursue economic livelihood strategies across borders, migrants will turn to clandestine methods. The predictable result has been a massive 'trade' in forged documentation and police corruption as migrants buy the right to stay, an increase in trafficking and the disintegration of sound and professional management practices.

In terms of forced migration, both Mozambique and latterly Angola have experienced major outflows of refugees to neighbouring countries and significant internal displacement. In Mozambique, for example, the civil war is estimated to have produced 4 million IDP's and a further 1.5 million refugees.[255] In the 1990s, the majority of refugees to Malawi, Swaziland and Zimbabwe retuned home but not without considerable uncertainty and hardship. Not so the 350,000 refugees who fled from southern Mozambique to South Africa, many of whom remained.

In the 1990s, there has been a new and steady southward flow of forced migrants, undocumented migrants and students. South Africa now boasts sizable Francophone African and Nigerian urban communities.[256] Between 1994 and 2001, 64,000 applications were made for refugee status in South Africa. Foremost amongst these were applicants from the African countries of DRC (7,700), Angola (6,900), Somalia (5,900), Nigeria (5,300), Senegal (4,500), Ethiopia (3,200) and Burundi (2,000), and the Asian countries of India (6,400), Pakistan (5,300) and Bangladesh (1,300).

Refugee determination is heavily influenced by national origin, as reflected in acceptance rates. Somali applicants had a 90 per cent success rate, Angolans 65 per cent, DRC 64 per cent, and Burundi 46 per cent. On the other hand, Indian applicants have an 88 per cent rejection rate, closely followed by Nigeria (82 per cent), Senegal (82 per cent), and Bangladesh (72 per cent). Traffickers have battened on to this movement and sought to profit by it.[257] Other organizations have suggested that intra-regional trafficking for sexual exploitation is a growing cause for concern.[258]

SADC does not have a coordinated regional response to the challenge of internal and external refugee movements. Individual countries are left to shoulder the burden as best they can with support from international agencies. All are signatories to the major refugee conventions but few have advanced or adequate systems of refugee determination in place. Regional burden-sharing is a key concept that SADC could easily turn into a reality.

Migration in Southern Africa is profoundly gendered. In the colonial period, women were generally prohibited from migrating. As the primary reasons for migration in the region have been for labour, men have dominated internal and cross-border migration. Today women and men are differently involved in and affected by migration. Although women are increasingly part of the movement of skilled migrants in the region and out of it, and have proportionally higher educational levels than male migrants, they are more likely to be involved in less skilled and informal work and therefore may be more likely to be irregular migrants, with the attendant disadvantages, as it is harder for them to access legal migration channels.[259]

Women are migrants in their own right, as well as partners of migrant male spouses.[260] Notwithstanding this, a recent study found that male respondents were more likely to have been to South Africa than female (Mozambique: 41 per cent of men and 9 per cent of women; Zimbabwe: 25 per cent and 20 per cent; Lesotho: 86 per cent and 76 per cent).[261] Traditional areas of employment for women migrants (internal and cross-border) have been agriculture (particularly seasonal work), domestic work, the service sector and trade. Men are more likely to have formal employment, particularly in the industrial (especially mining), agricultural and construction sectors.

The Southern African region is being increasingly integrated into transnational continental and regional trade networks, both formal and informal.[262] Informal traders or small entrepreneurs are amongst the most enterprising and energetic of contemporary migrants. They face major bureaucratic and other obstacles, even within a region heading for free trade by 2008. Trading is a key means of livelihood for many households in some countries and needs to be better understood and, wherever possible, facilitated by policy changes governing entrance, exit and customs duties. Work could also be done with traders and traders associations to build capacity, provide micro-finance and maximise the development spin-offs of informal trade.

All of the countries of SADC have experienced rapid post-independence urbanization, which, with few exceptions, has shown few signs of slowing. The primary evidence for rapid urbanization lies in census data. Unfortunately, with the exception of South Africa, national urbanization data is generally a decade or more old. However, as the results of the 2002 round of censuses become available, a relatively updated picture will emerge. Case study evidence has shown that:

- The lifting of colonial and apartheid restrictions on internal movement made a significant difference to many poor households who were freer to pursue livelihood strategies away from the rural areas.

- Rapid urbanization is largely a function of rural poverty. Environmental shocks, such as drought and flooding, have accelerated this process, as has the failure of the rural development industry and state agricultural policies to stabilise populations in the countryside.

- The displacement of poverty from the countryside to the town has led to new forms of survival strategy such as a greatly enlarged informal sector in most cities and the growth of urban agriculture. Both of these processes and the enabling policy responses they have provoked have been examined in considerable depth in many SADC countries.

- Rural-urban migration is not a one-time, all-inclusive process. The emergence and spread of the 'geographically-split household' is one of the major defining features of post-independence internal migration. Research in Namibia has demonstrated that new forms of rural-urban reciprocity have been underwritten by circulatory migration. Urban food security for the poor is predicated on the flow of remittances to the countryside and foodstuffs to the city.

- Most first-generation city-dwellers maintain strong rural linkages. However, there is growing evidence that the ties become much weaker with second- and third-generation in-migrants. The South African and Zambian cases suggest that such ties may eventually be severed altogether.

The clear implication of this seems to be that much greater attention should be focused on urban poverty and food security than happens at present and rather less on 'rural development' as traditionally conceived.

Urban poverty in some cities is prompting some reverse migration (de-urbanization) in countries such as Zambia. The viability and desirability of this as a livelihoods strategy is uncertain but depends critically on the viability of rural production and access to productive resources. In many countries of SADC, this trend could therefore accelerate in the future. In countries like South Africa and Lesotho it is highly unlikely.

4.3 Importance of Migration to the Poor

Cross-border and internal migration constitute significant livelihood strategies for Southern Africans across all skill levels. Internal and cross-border migration are integral to regional labour markets, and therefore, regional livelihood strategies. Migration has a strong relationship to poverty, social exclusion, as well as poverty alleviation.[263] Yet, there is little evidence of acknowledgement of these relationships (let alone migration itself) in national, donor, and international pro-poor policies.

Cross-border and internal migration takes many forms. Studies of cross-border migration show that circular migratory patterns are prevalent.[264] Thus, migrants may leave family members in their home country maintaining access to land and housing in rural and urban areas. Studies by SAMP indicate that regional cross-border migrants to South Africa say they have better access to land, housing and services in their home countries and that they are travelling for work and trading opportunities. Migration is, therefore, a way to amass capital and income. Maintaining two homes may be expensive, but it enables migrants to retain access to land and housing.

For similar reasons, circular migration is also a feature of internal migration. In South Africa, apartheid restrictions on movement and settlement enforced the development of circular migration. Studies indicate that the most common form of internal migrancy in the region has been rural-urban. Rural-urban migration of individuals and families reflects opportunities available in urban areas and pressure on land in rural areas.

Surprisingly, given levels of migration, data on the remittance behaviour of internal and cross-border migrants and receiving households is limited. Similarly, little information is available on their impact on national economies, economic development, alleviating inequalities, and on financial systems in the region. Furthermore, remittances in the form of goods are not recorded. And, little is known about any differences in the remittance behaviour of male and female migrants. SAMP is currently undertaking an eight-country study on remittance behaviour and household livelihoods.

Data on cash remittances is hard to gather as foreign exchange regulations, weak financial infrastructures and high transfer costs in formal systems encourage the use of informal channels for transferring money. This is because:

- Formal banking systems can be difficult and expensive to access.

- Getting a bank account is hard for low-income earners and semi-literate people.

- Transfer costs in formal banking systems can be higher than in informal systems, especially for small amounts.

- Many areas (particularly rural) are not serviced by formal banking systems.[265]

- Irregular cross-border migrants often cannot access formal transfer systems.

- Foreign exchange regulations and differential exchange rates may inhibit the use of formal systems, e.g. Zimbabwean cross-border migrants are unlikely to use formal channels as official exchange rates are far below black market exchange rates.[266]

National level data on cross-border and internal remittances are largely unavailable. However, in 2001 in Lesotho, remittances were estimated to contribute as much as 26.5 per cent of GDP.[267] A significant proportion of this comes from mineworkers. To encourage remittances, under bilateral agreements, Lesotho and Mozambican mineworkers receive part of their pay as deferred pay. Therefore, a portion of their pay is compulsorily sent to their home country where it is collected. Mozambican mineworkers can also take advantage of reduced tariffs on goods ordered and sent home by a specific company. Other than these schemes, there is no evidence of government policies to encourage remittance transfer. Non-national mineworkers on the South African mines can use a bank run by the main recruiting company, TEBA bank, to transfer funds.

For national economies, cross-border remittances are a source of foreign exchange and taxes, contribute to the balance of payments, and provide capital for enterprises and household investment.[268] Global research on remittance flows shows that in developing countries they are exceeded only by foreign direct investment, and exceed donor and capital market flows, and are more stable.[269] Given the high rates of migrancy in the region, it is possible that the same holds true in Southern Africa. Furthermore, remittances go directly to households. Remittances from internal migrants spatially redistribute income and relieve some income distribution inequalities.

Remittances to home areas contribute to household livelihoods. Remittances may be in goods or cash. Remittances can play a key role in the livelihoods of migrant households allowing for social, or human capital investment in education, health and housing and food. They may also be used as capital to invest in income-earning household inputs as well as to capitalise entrepreneurial activities. It is commonly held that remittances flow from migrants in urban areas to rural households. However, research from Namibia on internal migration suggests that remittances promoting food security may be a two-way flow.[270]

To enable migrant households to make the most of their earnings, it appears there is a need for affordable, accessible banking systems available in rural and urban areas and which can handle international transfers. Further research is required to understand the needs of migrants for channels to remit money and goods effectively so best use can be made of remittances once they are received. Assistance with the development of effective, safe banking systems and foreign exchange regulations which can accommodate low-income earners and which meet international requirements (e.g. FATF) are required.

Informal sector cross-border trade is important to the transfer of goods and commodities in the region. Initial studies of cross-border trade in the region suggest that:

- It is significant to the movement of food and agricultural goods in the region;

- It plays a role in regional food security;

- It plays a part in the development of small and medium enterprises;

- It is a household livelihood strategy;

- It engages a significant number of women;

- It constitutes a significant proportion of cross-border traffic in the region;

- Policymakers have yet to engage with this trade.[271]

Cross-border traders are also involved in other entrepreneurial activities in the region. Initial research in South Africa suggests they bring skills and employment opportunities for nationals.[272]

However, more needs to be known and understood about the extent of informal sector cross-border trade in the region and its role in livelihood strategies and food security, as well as an income-earning opportunity for women. Further research is required to better understand the relationship between these entrepreneurs and their businesses, poverty alleviation, agricultural commodity and consumption chains and food security. This research could inform the development of migration, trade, and investment policies which include these entrepreneurs and that could promote the positive aspects of this sector and ameliorate the negative. Furthermore, it could inform the development of training programmes for participants to enable them to develop their businesses as well as the development of facilitating financial systems.

Research suggests that cross-border trading provides a significant income-earning opportunity for women, who constitute a significant proportion of informal sector cross-border traders. However, neither migration legislation, nor regional and national trade policies, accommodate the activities of cross-border traders.[273]

Women migrants were more likely to be disadvantaged by the migration experience than their male counterparts. They are more likely to be single or widowed, but less likely to be in formal sector employment or to own property than their male counterparts.[274] Migration is a significant livelihood strategy for women and women-headed households.[275] Although women constitute a significant part of cross-border and internal migratory movement, they are also left behind as employment and earning opportunities favour men.

The wives and family members of migrants (internal and cross-border) may be left behind to retain access to land and housing in home areas, as well as to pursue traditional household activities. This increases the labour load of the home household, and, as remittances may be intermittent, can place house-holds in a precarious position, and encourage unsafe sexual behaviour. On the other hand, regular remittances may provide inputs to the household.

Little is known about the internal or cross-border migration of children as migrants or refugees. However, they may migrate in their own right or with parents to work as child labourers, particularly in the agricultural sector. SAMP research suggests that cross-border migrants prefer to leave children behind. A study by Save the Children Fund South Africa, found an increase in the number of unaccompanied Zimbabwean children entering South Africa in 2003 for work in the northern border areas as a result of economic crisis and drought. Census 2001 suggests that, in South Africa at least, internal migrants are likely to travel with their children.[276] This may be to enable access to better schooling.

While some attempts have been made to better understand the gender dimensions of migration, the area remains unexplored. In a changing migra-tion arena, affected by changing roles for women, employment opportunities, household structure as well as HIV/AIDS, further contemporary research into the impact of migration on gender as well as household formation and liveli-hood strategies could assist policymakers in the development of effective poverty alleviation strategies. Furthermore, more needs to be known about the impact of migration on the lives of children, their education, their health, and their access to health services.

Links between HIV/AIDS, migration and poverty are close and complex.[277] The current geography of the epidemic is also the clue to its link with mobil-ity. The highest incidence is not in Africa's poorest countries, but in Southern African countries such as South Africa and Botswana which have good trans-port infrastructure, relatively high levels of economic development, and con-siderable internal and cross-border migration. Understanding this region can therefore help in the prediction – and thus prevention – of the spread of HIV elsewhere on the African continent.

There are four key ways in which migration is tied to the rapid spread and high prevalence of HIV/AIDS:

- There is a higher rate of infection in 'migrant communities', which are often socially, economically and politically marginalised.

- Migrants' multi-local social networks create opportunity for mobile sexual networking.

- Mobility per se can encourage or make people vulnerable to high-risk sexual behaviour.

- Mobility makes people more difficult to reach through interventions, whether for preventive education, condom provision, HIV testing, or post-infection treatment and care.

There is abundant empirical evidence of a link between HIV/AIDS and mobility. The incidence of HIV has been found to be higher near roads, and amongst people who either have personal migration experience or have sexual partners who are migrants. In Southern Africa, migrant workers (and their sexual partners) have a higher level of infection than the general population. Itinerant traders display high infection rates and the infection rate is spectacularly high amongst truck drivers and migrant sex workers. Refugees and internally displaced persons have also been found to be especially vulnerable to HIV infection. Different forms of migration lead to different social and geographical forms of migrant 'community', and thus to different risk.

Looking at the relationship from the other direction, it is apparent that HIV/AIDS will become an increasingly important factor influencing migration and mobility and household sustainability in Africa:

- People with AIDS commonly return to live with family members to obtain care. This might entail moving from an urban back to a rural area or from one country to another. Others migrate in order to provide care to family members living elsewhere.

- Loss of a household's income though death or debilitation of a former migrant worker encourages migration by other household members to seek income-earning opportunities. As most migrants today are still male, this could lead to an increase in female migration.

- Death or debilitation of household or community members can lead to a decline in rural productivity and food security, thus contributing to pressure for out-migration by remaining members.

- High rates of death or debilitation in particular labour sectors create the need to replace workforce with new migrant workers. (This is one factor that may explain the 'Mozambicanization' of the South African mine labour force, as employers seek out labour from areas known to have lower HIV infection rates.)

- People diagnosed HIV-positive or displaying physical evidence of disease may migrate to avoid stigmatisation by their community.

- People with AIDS-related opportunistic infections migrate to obtain health care. This could involve cross-border movements to a country perceived to have better health care facilities.

- The HIV/AIDS death toll disproportionately affects the most economically productive strata of society in some countries. Skills gaps and shortages could lead countries to seek replacement skills from other African countries. The result would be an increase in brain drain within Africa. AIDS orphans (who may themselves be HIV positive) migrate to live with relatives or to seek their own income-earning opportunities.

- New widows or widowers (also themselves often HIV positive) may migrate upon the death of their partner. Women or men may choose to move after the death of a spouse, perhaps to rejoin biological family elsewhere. The death of a husband can lead to wife losing access to land and thus a livelihood, forcing her to move elsewhere to seek a living.

- HIV/AIDS is placing an increasing burden on rural communities, not only in terms of care of returning migrants but also in declining agricultural production and productivity.

HIV/AIDS may also impede certain forms of migration. For example, parents dying today means that there will be no grandparents for the next generation of children, and grandparents have traditionally been important in caring for children while parents migrated in search of employment. HIV/AIDS creates new motives for migrating while making some established forms of migration more difficult to sustain.

Migration is the means by which many African individuals and households seek income and livelihood security. Migration is a critical factor in understanding the epidemiology of HIV/AIDS including the incidence and prevalence of the epidemic. Migration has also emerged as a critical incidental and strategic response to coping with the consequences of the disease. However, to recognise the existence of these connections is insufficient. More knowledge, based on sound research, is needed to identify the links and their implications for migration policy and the effective management of HIV/AIDS.

4.4 International Migration and the Brain Drain

The 'brain drain' issue is a recurrent theme in the Southern African media, with much heat, little light and a great deal of scaremongering. The brain drain is increasingly cited as the cause of a growing skills crisis in individual countries and the region as a whole.[278] In South Africa, the idea of a brain drain-induced 'skills crisis' was the single most significant reason for the recent rethink of government policy towards skills immigration. Is there a 'skills crisis' brought on by a combination of skills emigration and restrictive immigration policy? Despite the extraordinarily poor quality of the data, there can be little doubt that the 'brain drain' has accelerated from the SADC region since 1990, particularly from South Africa and Zimbabwe. Domestically, economic and political circumstances have conspired to create a large pool of potential emigrants. New global job opportunities in many sectors have turned latency into action.

The brain drain has undoubtedly accelerated in the last decade but some care is required in interpreting data and making policy recommendations for the following reasons:

- Uncertainty over the numbers involved. In the case of South Africa, there is evidence that official statistics undercount the numbers by as much as two-thirds. Studies of other countries in the region show statistics that are either nonexistent or very badly outdated. In the vacuum, highly-inflated guesstimates are extremely common in the media.

- Most projections about future trends are based on faulty methodological assumptions that tend to exaggerate the likelihood of emigration.

- There is a common notion that emigration means departure for good. Many who depart do not intend to stay away permanently. And, consistent with the precepts of transnationalism, those that leave retain strong backward linkages.

- A distinction must be made between a sizable intra-regional brain drain and emigration from the region. Some countries are disadvantaged by both (Zimbabwe). Some may gain what others lose (South Africa, Botswana). For the region as a whole, within-SADC brain drain means no net loss.

- The 'demand' side means that some sectors are harder hit than others.

- There is little concrete evidence about the actual economic and social impact of the brain drain, even in sectors hardest hit.

- The reality is that most countries in the region have eschewed 'brain gain' strategies in the form of proactive immigration policies and search for replacement skills. The impact of the brain drain of citizens is exacerbated as a result.[279]

Clearly, all governments would benefit from an improved baseline capacity to document and monitor the extent of skills emigration.

A systematic data base of the numbers and skills profile of diasporic Southern Africans worldwide using host country census, immigration and survey data would also be an extremely useful exercise. In the absence of reliable statistics, prediction of future trends is also a hazardous exercise. SAMP developed a methodology in the late 1990s to assess the real emigration potential of the skilled population. At one end of the spectrum was Botswana with low rates of emigration and low emigration potential. At the other were South Africa and Zimbabwe. In the case of South Africa, an Emigration Potential Index was developed which showed 2 per cent of the skilled population with very high emigration potential (32,000 individuals), a further 10 per cent (192,000) with high potential, and 25 per cent with moderate potential. SAMP also initiated a six-country study of skills-in-training – the PSBS or Potential Skills Base Survey – to assess the emigration intentions and potential of tomorrow's labour force.

The brain drain in the health sector is clearly the most problematical for countries within the region. Aggressive recruiting of health professionals by Europe and North America is denuding the region of scarce skills, at a time when they can ill afford to lose them. Working conditions emerge as the single most important predisposing factor for health professional emigration.[280] As Loewenson and Thompson argue, 'personnel scarcities have become a critical limiting factor in health interventions' for the public health sector and the poorest populations.[281] Health systems in Southern Africa face a variety of problems, including 'an overall lack of personnel in key areas of the health sector; an inequitable distribution of those health personnel who are available (public v private, urban v rural); and a significant attrition of trained personnel from the health sector and from the region'. The capacity of the public health sector to deliver services is being compromised by the brain drain at precisely the time at which the HIV/AIDS epidemic is seriously increasing the burden on the system.

There are no adequate statistics to measure the existing stock of health professionals and the extent and trends in health personnel flows from and within the region or individual countries.[282] In the case of the health sector, two additional factors complicate any attempt to assess the stock of health professionals from local health council data. First, many who leave maintain local registration with the councils. Second, some who register no longer practice or practice on a part-time basis. In general, policy responses to the brain drain have been control-oriented in character and not informed by research on the actual perceptions and intentions of the skilled.

Various initiatives have sought to encourage the return of diasporic citizens by offering incentives and job-matching programmes. The IOM's Return and Reintegration of Qualified African Nationals (RQAN) Program (which included Angola, Mozambique and Zimbabwe within SADC) assisted the return of a miserly total of 2,009 professionals to Africa as a whole over a 17-year period. On the evidence of RQAN, these kinds of programmes are likely to be ineffectual at best. Recently, the IOM has initiated a more flexible skills transfer programme called MIDA (Migration for Development in Africa) with the IOM acting as a kind of 'go-between'. While this programme seems, in principle, to have a higher likelihood of success, its effectiveness has yet to be tested. In general, it seems likely that formalised skills return or linkage schemes coordinated by international organizations are not going to have a major impact in reversing or ameliorating the effects of the brain drain.

Although increasing attention has been given to the brain drain in Southern Africa, the field is notable for the lack of sound information on which to base policies that might impact positively on the poor. A more systematic and comprehensive effort needs to be made to:

- Document the extent of the brain drain by examining data in the region and in major host countries;

- Produce an inventory of the overseas skills base and, through survey work, determine the potential for return and the nature of backward linkages (financial and social);

- Systematically assess the economic impact and resource implications of the brain drain by sector (with particular emphasis on health implications for the poor); and

- Work with government and private industry to develop retention, replacement, brain train and attraction strategies to mitigate the impact of skills loss on development prospects.

4.5 Migration Policies

Migration policy is formulated at various interlocking scales from the continental (NEPAD) to the local (city government). A major challenge is how to get these different levels of governance to interface with one another to develop an integrated approach to policy development and migration management. A second challenge is to understand the institutional mechanisms and constraints operating on the development and implementation of policy.

At the continental level, NEPAD's attitude to the migration issue is emblematic. Freer movement of people across the continent is cited as a key long-term objective of the AU. Little analysis is presented of the reasons for this position and likely positive impacts and there is no systematic discussion of the institutional mechanisms by which this might be achieved. At the regional level, the Southern African Development Community (SADC) aims to promote regional development through cooperation and integration. Protocols pursuing these aims have been developed. In 2000, the SADC Free Trade Protocol was ratified. Attempts to move towards the free movement of people within the SADC have been less successful. Increasingly, regional realities demand that national governments consider whether or not to soften their borders and/or move towards a harmonised approach to migration management. Unfortunately, the

---

Box 16: Facilitating movement in Southern Africa

The countries of the SADC region are committed to greater regional integration in all economic spheres. They have been considerably more resistant to the idea that the freedom of movement of people in the region would hasten economic integration and regional development. National immigration policies are, almost without exception, focused on exclusion and control. Development is certainly not mainstreamed into immigration policy (and nor for that matter is migration mainstreamed into development and poverty reduction policy). The SADC Secretariat tabled a Protocol on Free Movement as long ago as 1995. Even a much-diluted Protocol on the Facilitation of Movement was consistently opposed by a group of countries led by South Africa. The issue remained deadlocked until 2002 when discussion resumed on the Facilitation Protocol. South Africa, with a new ANC Minister of Home Affairs in charge, reversed its earlier hostility to greater freedom of movement within SADC. When the Protocol was ratified by 6 states in 2005, South Africa was amongst the first countries to endorse it. The winds of change are blowing through South African migration policy after a decade of prevarication and indecision. Without doubt, the migration and development issue will soon come on to the policy agenda in that country, if not in the region as a whole.

Source: Oucho and Crush (2002); see endnote 283.

first attempt to craft a SADC-wide protocol on free movement ran aground on the rocks of opposition from South Africa, Botswana and Namibia.[283] In 1997, it was replaced by the more cautious Draft Protocol on the Facilitation of Movement of People. Even this Protocol was rejected in 2000 by the SADC Council of Ministers.[284]

Only in 2003 did the SADC Secretariat revive the Protocol. Whether the protocol will suffer a different fate second time round remains to be seen. However, the reality is that this Protocol, or one of similar ilk, would have major positive implications for the poor of the region, freeing up obstacles to cross-border movement and the search for a livelihood through migration.

In sum, unlike in other areas such as trade, education and transportation, there has been considerable reluctance to move forward on developing a SADC-wide policy on the movement of people. Cross-border migration in the region is, therefore, governed by national migration and refugee legislation.

COMESA, to which a number of SADC states belong, has been a little more positive about the concept of freer movement of persons within the borders of the grouping. There seems to be less opposition to the idea within COMESA, whose founding Treaty advocates the free movement of persons within the area. Acceptance of the principle was probably facilitated by the fact that South Africa is not a member. How this will be operationalised, however, is unclear.

In the aftermath of the collapse of the Protocol, SAMP and the IOM combined to establish the Migration Dialogue for Southern Africa (MIDSA) in partnership with all SADC states. MIDSA has become an established and well-recognised forum for training and policy debate on a variety of issues pertaining to migration management in the region. During 2003, the major development was the preparation by SAMP of a major report on migration policy harmonization within the SADC region. This report was presented and discussed at the November 2004 MIDSA Forum in Maseru, Lesotho. In 2005, MIDSA held a forum on migration and development which foregrounded the role of migration in poverty reduction for senior officials and policymakers in the region. Further forums will be convened thereafter, as the two organizations involved seek to move the migration issue even more firmly onto government agendas throughout the region.

In terms of national immigration policy, the overriding focus of most legal instruments is enforcement, control and exclusion. The particulars vary from country to country but the overall intent is extremely similar.[285] No country, with the possible exception of Botswana, has migrant or immigrant-friendly legislation on the books.[286] Most policies were devised in the immediate post-colonial period. The imperatives of new nation-building and Africanization did not encourage the idea of immigration as a tool of social and economic development. Indeed, outsiders were generally viewed as a threat to citizens. Legal stays were time-limited and goal-directed. Permanent immigration is extremely difficult from one country to another within the SADC and into the region from outside. Tanzania and Zambia are currently undergoing a process of immigration policy reform. Opportunity therefore exists in those countries to integrate pro-poor considerations into the legislation.

All countries within SADC are adopting an increasingly harsh line on enforcement. In South Africa, human rights lawyers have argued that many enforcement tactics are strongly reminiscent of the apartheid pass laws and influx controls.[287] A corruption industry has sprung up as the enforcers are paid off for the right to remain.[288] There has been a major increase in deportations since the end of apartheid. Since 1990, South Africa has deported over one million people to neighbouring countries, 70 per cent of these to Mozambique (including many former refugees). Other countries are beginning to follow suit, particularly Botswana in regard to undocumented Zimbabweans in the country. The workability of this deportation system is dubious and does not justify the cost. All it appears to do is enrich the enforcers and disrupt the lives and livelihoods of the deportees. People using migration as a livelihood can scarcely afford the disruption to lives and livelihoods that usually ensues.

At the national level, Mozambique, Namibia, South Africa and Zimbabwe have all made significant changes to migration laws in the past ten years and Lesotho, Tanzania and Malawi are currently revising their legislation.[289] Only the immigration legislation of South Africa and Mozambique makes any reference to complying with international conventions, and bilateral accords.[290] Arrest, detention and repatriation procedures do not always protect irregular (and regular) migrants from abuse.[291] Furthermore, they have the potential to cause conflict between neighbouring countries.

As in most parts of the world, immigration legislation favours the entry of skilled and wealthy migrants. However, the legislation and migration policy of the region still hampers the recruitment of skilled professionals to replace those who are being lost. Bilateral agreements and legislation allow the South African mining and agricultural sectors to employ contract migrant workers from neighbouring countries.[292] A number of other agreements exist at bilateral levels between countries in the region to facilitate or hamper movement. As noted above, bilateral agreements exist around skilled migration. For instance, the United Kingdom has agreed that it will not directly recruit medical professionals and teachers. There is little evidence that such measures are effective. The UK is considering direct assistance to Malawi to slow the loss of medical professionals from the country.

Associated with the liberation struggle, and civil war in Mozambique, forced migration has long been a feature of the region. All countries under discussion have ratified or comply with the 1951 Convention Relating to the Status of Refugees and the more inclusive 1969 OAU Convention Governing the Specific Aspects of Refugee Problems in Africa.[293] The Refugee Acts of Mozambique, Namibia, South Africa and Zimbabwe incorporate both definitions of refugees.[294] The Botswana Refugee Act restricts its definition to that under the 1951 Convention.[295] Swaziland's and Zambia's refugee legislation gives the Minister the power to define a refugee, but in practice they are guided by the 1951 and 1969 Conventions. Botswana is said to reject asylum claims from people from outside the region.[296]

The Refugee Acts of Lesotho, Malawi, Mozambique, Namibia, South Africa and Zimbabwe protect asylum seekers from non-refoulement, do not require them to meet immigration legislation requirements for entry, and give recognised refugees the right to remain in the country.[297] Although not protected by legislation, these principles are largely upheld in practice by Swaziland and Zambia. Ministers of Lesotho, Malawi, South Africa, Swaziland, Zambia and Zimbabwe can declare a class of persons to be refugees. Individual status determination procedures are found in all the countries under discussion.

With the exception of South Africa, by law and in practice, countries in the region require refugees and asylum seekers to live in designated areas (usually some form of camp), and Zambia allows some exceptions to this rule.[298] With the exception of Mozambique and South Africa, refugees and asylum seekers are required to apply for work permits before they can work.[299] Refugees in Mozambique, South Africa, Swaziland, Zambia and Zimbabwe are entitled to some form of identity and travel documents. As support to refugees and asylum seekers is limited in the region, the rights to freedom of movement and work are important. Differences in refugee and asylum policies are significant and harmonisation of policy could establish minimum standards. More needs to be known about how refugees and asylum seekers survive, as well as their actual potential contributions and costs to receiving countries.

No country in the region has specific legislation regarding trafficking, and existing legislation makes no provisions for the protection of trafficked persons. However, South Africa is considering anti-trafficking legislation.[300] Given the lack of attention paid to trafficking it is unclear how prevalent the problem is in the region. However, evidence suggests that women and children are trafficked for sexual purposes.[301] There is also anecdotal evidence that irregular migrants pay couriers to facilitate and guide entry, particularly across land borders, but that these migrants are not trafficked.

All countries in Southern Africa have ratified the Convention on the Rights of the Child. Botswana, Lesotho, Malawi, Namibia and South Africa have signed the associated Protocol on the Rights of the Child in Armed Conflict. And, Botswana, Malawi, Mozambique, Namibia and South Africa have all signed the associated Protocol on the sale of children, child prostitution, and child pornography. While most countries have legislation that outlaws child labour and protects children from exploitation, their ability to enforce such legislation is doubtful.

The UNHCR and UNICEF operate in all countries in the region. Other international agencies tasked with the protection of vulnerable groups also operate in the region, for instance, the Save the Children Fund. These agencies do not have a specific mandate to protect migrants or promote migrant rights. Perhaps reflecting the migration environment, it seems it is only in South Africa that NGOs and church-based organisations specifically attempt to protect migrants, but focus on refugees and asylum seekers.[302] Trade Unions and other professional organisations may also protect the rights of legal migrant workers.

The principle of freer movement within the SADC region is critically important. So too is the idea that policies should be harmonised. Despite the political sensitivities, the status quo simply cannot prevail. Existing national migration frameworks are not integrated into poverty reduction strategy. For migration to become a lever of social and economic upliftment for the poor, the migration issue has to be confronted at both national and regional levels.

The failure to craft a regionally-coordinated approach to migration in the 1990s is attributable to the concerns of migrant-receiving countries such as South Africa. It is inevitable that SADC will be forced to confront the issue again. The scale of unrecorded migration and the attendant exploitation of migrants require a coordinated response. Freeing up flows of goods and capital while simultaneously trying to shut down the movement of people makes limited economic sense. And if nothing else makes countries reconsider their need to import labour from their neighbours, the HIV/AIDS epidemic will eventually do it for them.

In 2004-5, the Draft Protocol on Facilitation of Movement within SADC was revisited and ratified by six states. Regional dialogue on this and other issues is essential. MIDSA is the only high-level, intergovernmental forum designed to catalyze policy discussion and debate on the desirability and obstacles of a regional approach to migration management. MIDSA forums and technical workshops are attended by representatives from all 14 SADC states and provide an important venue for identifying national obstacles and opportunities for a regionally-coordinated approach. The hope is that MIDSA will eventually be absorbed into SADC and that the forum will have very direct impacts on the harmonization of national immigration laws and data collection systems.

Assistance with harmonising migration legislation and data collection could promote more effective management of migration in the region. To promote effective implementation of legislation and to curtail corruption, further research is required on the training needs of Departments of Immigration, and with training of officials. Further research is also needed on the effectiveness of arrest and detention procedures across the region and their impact on regional relationships.

In terms of improved service delivery to the poor (citizens and non-citizens) there is an urgent need to professionalise the activities of Departments of Home Affairs and Immigration throughout the region.

Migration has not been systematically factored into national poverty reduction strategies throughout the region. Nor has immigration policy been integrated systematically with pro-poor policies. Most immigration and migration policy frameworks were developed before the contemporary focus on poverty reduction began to frame foreign aid and state policy. On the other hand, it is apparent that few poverty reduction strategies (as evidenced by PRSPs, etc.) have made any serious attempt to integrate migration realities into strategising and planning. Hence there is a profound disjuncture between immigration policies and poverty reduction strategies in most countries of the Southern African region.

Xenophobia and hostility to migrants is common in the region, and in some countries (e.g. South Africa) can involve physical attacks on non-nationals. A SAMP study suggests that nationals of Botswana, Namibia, and South Africa are particularly intolerant of non-nationals, and especially African non-nationals.[303] These attitudes are reflected in the media and often in government policies and the rhetoric of politicians. The new South African Immigration Act commits the government to challenge xenophobia; however, it is difficult to know how it will do so. The UNHCR and the South African Human Rights Commission are funding a Roll Back Xenophobia Campaign, which provides limited training to relevant officials, journalists and schools.

High levels of xenophobia are of concern, not just because they make individual migrants' lives uncomfortable. Xenophobia allows the exclusion of non-nationals from vital services that they may be entitled to, for instance, health and education, and further marginalises and excludes vulnerable communities, thus increasing inequalities – even for non-nationals who are in the country legally.[304] Furthermore, while the regulatory regime looks relatively protective of migrants, immigrants, refugees and asylum seekers, most governments (including wealthier countries like South Africa) lack the resources to effectively enforce legislation.

More also needs to be known about the access and exclusion of migrants, adults and children, to services to which they may be entitled. Combined with research on xenophobia, this could assist in curriculum development for schools and training programmes which could be used to educate people and service providers on the rights and entitlements of different categories of migrants.

Despite the importance of both cross-border and internal migration to the region, pro-poor policies of governments, the region and continent, as well as donor agencies and countries that include migrants, are lacking. Internal and cross-border migrants appear to be operating in a policy environment that largely excludes them, although they may, in some cases, be affected by these policies. Regional migration policies, legislation and practice are fragmented along national lines, and at times do not appear to meet the objectives of contemporary regional and continental policies of the SADC, COMESA, or NEPAD. And, they often seem to omit the needs of migrants and possibilities for developing managed migration regimes, whether regional or nationally based, that could allow migrants, and national economies, to maximise the possibilities of regional migration and minimise the negative impacts.

On a continental level, NEPAD, an initiative by African governments to stimulate and promote the development of Africa and its peoples, like national and regional development policies, is silent around issues of migration. While the development of programmes and policies under NEPAD is still in its early stages, the only real mention of migration concerns the movement of skilled professionals, and particularly health professionals. Yet, throughout the continent migration is a feature of African livelihoods and provides opportunities for development, as well as potential for conflict between African countries, which could undermine the principles of NEPAD. Understanding the role of migration across, through and from the continent could assist in the development of NEPAD policies, and in the stated intention to foster African cooperation, unity, interaction and development.

On a regional level, the SADC is intent on fostering regional integration and cooperation for development and the alleviation of poverty. The Regional

Indicative Strategic Development Plan (RISDP) does not, however, explicitly identify migration as a key area for community intervention. A close reading of the RISDP reveals that migration is a significant cross-cutting in all priority areas. The RISDP identifies numerous migration-related policy issues and concerns that the community will confront including the brain drain, informal trade, mobility of the 'factors of production', tourism, and so on. Hence there is every reason to suppose that SADC does recognise the significance of migration in poverty reduction and region policy integration. Migration has also resurfaced on the agenda of the SADC in the form of renewed attention to the Draft Protocol on the Facilitation of Movement of People.

Migration (internal and cross-border) is a key feature of the regional labour market and livelihood strategies of Southern Africans. A key pillar of SADC, the Free Trade Protocol, did not take into account that SMEs and small entrepreneurs are a key feature of regional trade. Their movement and income-generating possibilities are often constrained by national migration policies (even if unintentionally).

The Millenium Development Goals, PRSPs, and CAPs increasingly structure donor agency interventions in the region. To the extent that migration is sidelined or ignored in policy thinking, so pro-poor policy frameworks will fall short in their attempts to alleviate poverty and minimise inequalities in the region. Yet, they have the potential to make a significant difference to the lives of migrants and non-migrants. However, there are increasing signs that donor agencies are beginning to recognise the significance of migration as a development issue. CIDA and DFID support for the Southern African Migration Project is a case in point, as is EU and SIDA support for the HIV/AIDS and Mobility initiative, PHAMSA.

Migration has an impact on the following areas of policy formation and interventions to alleviate poverty, reduce inequality and to promote good governance:

- **Support to regional organisations**, e.g. SADC, COMESA. If migration is key to the region, and an unspoken part of regional cooperation and integration, efforts need to be made to integrate and mainstream migration when providing assistance to regional organisations in the development of policies, protocols and initiatives to reduce poverty, reduce inequalities and encourage development.

- **PRSP support models and some aspects of CAPs.** Where these are pursued, the links to migration can seem tenuous. Yet, if the PRSP is to be effective, should the role of migration in the country's economy and poverty alleviation policies not be considered? Providing support to governments in the preparation and implementation of budgets may seem rather remote from migration and other PRSP support activities. But consideration needs to be given to:

- Understanding the role of migration in a country's fiscus;

- Quantifying remittances as part of GNP;

- Identifying the role of remittances at national, regional/provincial, local and household levels;

- Identifying the role (and its potential role) of migrant incomes in tax regimes;

- Identifying the role of migration in key areas of budgetary activity, e.g. health, education, infrastructure, agriculture, to ensure spending is appropriate;

- Identifying the impact of migration on service delivery;

- Identifying the impact of skilled emigration on service provision and staffing and training demands;

- Identifying the impact of migration on demand for services (which may change according to seasonal patterns of migration (e.g. agricultural labour) or to changes in employment opportunities elsewhere (e.g. retrenchments in South African mines);

- Identifying where migrant populations are particularly vulnerable, or alleviating poverty to target spending appropriately;

- Identifying the role of migration and income through migration in taxation.

- **Governance**. Governance programmes include minimising corruption in administrations. The SADC and NEPAD show the commitment of most governments in the region to developing good governance. Territorial integrity and security are key to most nation states. Migration (and associated customs and excise issues) is an area of concern for both security, and corruption.

  - Anti-corruption initiatives should include Departments of Immigration/ Home Affairs, Trade and Industry, Customs and Excise as well as security services to ensure not only territorial integrity, but integrity in the implementation of migration and customs and excise legislation.

  - Governance in these areas should promote good management of migration, and not disadvantage (even if unintentionally) the positive poverty alleviating aspects of migration.

There is also a need for further research into governance aspects of migration including: developing appropriate anti-corruption programmes, service delivery and security.

- **Financial services.** Part of support to PRSPs, and development of governance policies includes assistance with the growth of secure, accessible financial services, which for some countries includes compliance with FTF. The role of remittances in development in the region, at national, regional and household levels is significant, and, as noted above, in some countries exceeds FDI. The use of informal banking and money transfer systems may have the potential to undermine efforts under FTF, and the growth of formal banking systems.

  - When developing assistance programmes to financial services, small investors, and individuals who wish to bank or accumulate relatively small amounts of money need to be accommodated.

  - Efforts need to be made to ensure that cross-border and internal transfers of relatively small amounts of money can be made with low transfer costs, to ensure the safe transfer of remittances while addressing security needs.

  - Development of other financial transfer systems that meet FTF requirements but are accessible to rural areas is needed.

  Further research is needed in the development of appropriate, accessible and affordable financial systems, including credit at regional and national levels, which promote pro-poor investment and the transfer and positive use of remittances and can accommodate internal and cross-border migrants.

- **Livelihoods approach.** Internal and cross-border migration play a key role in livelihoods strategies of households in the region. When considering policies to enable Southern Africans to maximise their household livelihoods there is a need to:

  - Identify the role of migration in urban and rural livelihood strategies.

  - Identify how policies to manage migration may affect urban and rural livelihoods.

  - Identify how other policies and economic changes may affect the livelihoods of migrant households.

There is a need to promote further research on the role of migration in household livelihood strategies to facilitate households maximising opportunities, as well as the role of remittances as part of livelihoods at regional, national, and local levels.

- **Rural development**. Internal and cross-border migrants constitute a significant proportion of the workforce in the commercial agricultural sector. Migration may affect small holder agricultural production at a household level. Internal and cross-border trade, which involve short-term migration, and for cross-border traders negotiation of migration controls, play an important role in the distribution of agricultural goods in the region, and in the livelihoods of producers. There is therefore a need to:

  - Identify the role of migrant labour in the viability of commercial agriculture, including the conditions and terms of employment of migrant labourers.

  - Identify how changes in the commercial agricultural sector may affect demands for labour, patterns of migrancy, and therefore the livelihoods of migrant households.

  - Identify the role of remittances in agricultural inputs for smallholder producers, and therefore the impact of policies which may cause changes in patterns of migrancy.

  Further research is needed on: migrancy, labour and commercial agriculture; role of remittances in smallholder agriculture; chains of commodity and consumption for agricultural goods in the region, including SME cross-border and internal trade; impact of direct and indirect barriers to trade; impact of changing employment opportunities on patterns of migrancy and agricultural production at a household level, and therefore poverty.

- **Food security**. As a livelihood strategy, migration obviously plays a role in food security. Changing patterns of migrancy may affect food security in some areas, e.g. large scale retrenchments in sectors employing migrant labour may affect food security in previously sending areas. Policies affecting patterns of trade and the movement of small entrepreneurs may have an impact on food security strategies. There is therefore a need to:

  - Identify the role of migration in food security strategies at a household level.

  - Identify how policies and economic changes which impact on migration may affect food security.

- Identify the role of trade and SME traders in food security.

There is also a need for further research on: the role of migration in food security in urban and rural areas at household level; the role of SME cross-border trade in the region in promoting or negatively impacting food security; and the impact of food security programmes on migration.

- **Infrastructure development**. Programmes concerned with the development of infrastructure may seem a long way from migration. However, who is the infrastructure being developed for? How does migration affect the demand for services (e.g. seasonally) and demographics of an area? Furthermore, infrastructure programmes (e.g. roads) may use migrant labour. Therefore to be effective, these programmes need to:

  - Account for migration and changing population distribution (including seasonal) when developing where and how much infrastructural development is required.

  - Identify where and how remittances may act as contributor to fees for the use of infrastructure or the tax base to pay for infrastructural development.

  - Identify the impact and implications of using migrant labour in the development of infrastructural programmes.

  - Design transport programmes to account for their use by migrants and SME traders.

- **Trade and customs and excise.** Trade ostensibly stands outside migration. Yet, a significant proportion of regional cross-border trade (and the majority across some borders), is undertaken by small entrepreneurs who migrate for short periods of time. They therefore have to negotiate the migratory legislative framework as well as customs and excise policies. Trade policies need to:

  - Account for the activities of SME, or informal sector, traders and their role in cross-border trade.

  - Promote SME trade as it has a direct impact on household livelihoods, the alleviation of poverty, and women's economic empowerment.

  - Encourage the positive aspects of informal sector, cross-border trade and ameliorate the negative.

  - Identify the impact of migration, trade and customs and excise policies and legislation on SME traders.

There is also a need for further research on: the role of informal and SME cross-border trade in regional trade; role of SME trade and the economic empowerment of women; role of the SME trade in entrepreneurial development; role of SME cross-border trade in household livelihoods; role of SME cross-border trade in agricultural commodity and consumption chains; role of SME cross-border trade in food security; role of migration regimes in encouraging or discouraging trade.

- **Service provision**. Migration has an impact on service delivery as the emigration of skilled professionals and others who deliver services affects investments in education (particularly at tertiary level), staffing levels, and training needs. It also affects the demand for services, gendered demand for services, and the kinds of services that might be required. For effective delivery of services there is a need to:

  - Identify levels of skilled migration to plan for future staffing needs and therefore demands for education, i.e. on service delivery and planning for future service delivery.

  - Identify the demand for services, and which services, by new in-migrants, internal and cross-border migrants.

  - Identify the impact of migration patterns on demand for services, by numbers, age, gender, and type of services.

  - Identify how patterns of migration affect demographics of an area and therefore demand for services in that location.

  There is also a need for further research on: the impact of migration on the use of services; if and how available services may act as a pull factor for migrants; whether migrants are excluded from access to essential services.

- **Education**. Education is central to the alleviation of poverty and development. Migration plays a role in the delivery and use of education. The emigration of teaching professionals in the region may affect the ability of government to effectively provide schooling. Migrant children (internal and cross-border) may change the spatial demand for educational services. Migrant children may be excluded from education. Therefore consideration needs to be given to:

  - Tracking and understanding the migration of teaching professionals within and outside the region to understand staffing needs.

  - Including retention and recruitment programmes for teachers in education budgets.

- Accounting for the use of education services by migrant children.

- Planning for recruitment and investment in tertiary education to ameliorate the loss of skills through emigration.

There is also a need for further research into: migration of education professionals; migrants and tertiary education; the use of education facilities by migrant children; the possible exclusion from education of migrant children; the use of remittances for education of children in migrant households.

- **Health.** Health is a key development indicator and poor health and health services a barrier to the alleviation of poverty. The emigration of health professionals, from nurses to surgeons, within and out of the region, is of great concern to regional governments. It affects the ability of governments to effectively deliver health services. People may migrate to take advantage of health services available in another place, or another country. There is a need to:

  - Track and understand the migration of health professionals and include in identifying staffing needs.

  - Include retention, recruitment and training programmes in health budgets.

  - Account for the use of health services by migrants.

  - Identify how new health policies may affect migration patterns.

There is also a need for further research including: quantification and understanding of the scope of emigration in the region; identifying what is pushing health professionals to migrate and what would assist in their retention; impact of emigration on service delivery in rural and urban areas; the role of health services in migration; the use of health services by migrants; the exclusion of migrants from health services; and the role of remittances in accessing health services for migrant households.

- **HIV/AIDS.** As discussed above, migration is a key feature of the epidemic in Southern Africa. It has played a role in the spread of HIV, and now the epidemic has a hold on the region, may affect migration patterns. So, effective HIV/AIDS education, prevention and treatment programmes need to:

  - Identify the role of migration in the epidemic in the country concerned.

  - Identify the impact of HIV/AIDS on current and future patterns of migration.

- Ensure programmes can accommodate the movements and needs of migrants, including basics such as developing evaluation mechanisms that can incorporate migrant populations.

- Ensure education and prevention programmes are accessible to migrants.

Further research is needed on HIV/AIDS and specific migrant populations, in specific countries; impact of HIV/AIDS on household livelihood strategies and consequently migration patterns; access to education, prevention and treatment programmes of migrants; impact of introduction of ARV programmes on migration patterns and therefore households.

- **Gender mainstreaming.** Migration is a gendered process. Evidence suggests that women constitute an increasing proportion of the migrant flow in Southern Africa, at all skill levels. It also suggests women may experience migration differently. Gender sensitive policies which are considering migration, and which may have an impact on migration need:

  - To identify how legislation (including migration legislation) may have a different impact on male and female migrants.

  - To identify the role of migration in women's economic and social empowerment – or disempowerment.

Further research is needed on the migration of women across the region, including: legislative and other barriers; cross-border traders; role of migration and remittances in the livelihoods of women 'left behind'; the role of migration in the empowerment or disempowerment of women, and particularly women-headed households.

The above discussion identifies the role that migration plays in key areas of development policy in the region and makes recommendations for considering migration when developing these policies. The existing policy frameworks of NEPAD, the SADC, national governments and donor agencies, including the MDGs, PRSPs, and CAPs provide opportunities to mainstream and retrofit migration. This chapter suggests there is a need to review these policies and initiatives to incorporate migration to enable them to more effectively intervene to reduce poverty and encourage development in the region. Notwithstanding the evidence of the role of migration in the lives of Southern Africans presented here, this paper also identifies gaps in knowledge which require further research to better enable policymakers to make and deliver effective poverty alleviation interventions.

The country summaries that follow use the same format as the regional report. However, the focus here is very selective. First, the major features of each national migration regime are presented. Second, the summaries focus on particular migration-related issues that are specific to the country concerned and/or of pressing policy importance. Third, the discussion highlights issues, such as the brain drain, common to all countries. The major finding in all countries is that despite some acknowledgement of the importance of migration to poor households, none of the current round of policy reduction strategies systematically integrates migration into their findings and recommendations. The result is a significant lacuna at the heart of poverty reduction strategies in Southern Africa. Migration needs to be systematically mainstreamed into all aspects of government and international agency efforts to reduce poverty and inequality. Ordinary people throughout the region view migration as a critical strategy for poverty reduction and community-level development. There is no reason why interventions designed to provide an enabling policy environment should not do the same.

4.6 South Africa

4.6.1 Introduction

South Africa is the major foreign migrant receiving country in the region. The overall number of 'visitors' to South Africa from other countries in the region rose significantly with the collapse of apartheid, from around 500,000 in 1990 to 5 million p.a. at the present time. The 2001 Census showed the total foreign-born population of South Africa as 1,025,072 including 687,678 from the SADC region, 228,318 from Europe and only 41,817 from the rest of Africa. These figures are sharply at odds with other estimates. Estimates of the numbers of undocumented migrants in South Africa have grown from the barely plausible to the completely outrageous: in the 1-2 million range in the early 1990s to 8-10 million at the present time.[305] President Mbeki claimed in January 2004 that there were 7 million 'illegal immigrants' and 3 million Zimbabweans in South Africa, figures without any basis in fact. One study claims that there are 500,000 Mozambican migrant workers, mostly in South Africa.[306] Another suggested in 2001 that a total of 400,000 Zimbabweans were in South Africa, most for work.[307] The primary reason for the census discrepancy is South Africa's large undocumented migrant population and the reluctance of foreign Africans to disclose their origins to the authorities.

Certainly there are more than 41,817 Africans from outside SADC in the country; but precisely how many is anyone's guess.

There has been a vigorous debate in South Africa about the numbers of undocumented migrants in the country. Official estimates, based on a methodologically dubious study by the HSRC, suggest numbers in the 4-8 million range. Despite the withdrawal of the study by the HSRC, officials continue to cite these figures as 'methodologically scientific'. Other studies have pointed out that the category of 'undocumented migrant' needs to be disaggregated into at least three streams: lawful entrants/unlawful stayers, unlawful entrants/lawful stayers; unlawful entrants/unlawful stayers. This, and other studies, point out that the 'unauthorised' population is a floating one, that it has been decreased by over 250,000 as a result of immigration amnesties between 1996-2000; and that the majority of migrants enter the country through legal means. South Africans believe that 25 per cent of the population is foreign. The figure is probably closer to 3-5 per cent with around 500,000 undocumented migrants.

Regardless of the numbers, the policy discourse around migration remains focused on the 'illegal alien' problem and how to deal with the obvious contradictions. For migrants from the region, migration to South Africa is a well-established household poverty reduction strategy. Legalised migration would make the benefits even more transparent and attainable since South African employers are known to favour foreign migrants in many sectors.

The apartheid system was predicated on the control of internal migration by black South Africans. So draconian were these controls (pass laws and influx controls) that scholars concluded that South Africa was characterised by 'constrained' or 'displaced' urbanization. The assumption, therefore, was that the collapse of apartheid would precipitate mass rural to urban movement. Census data shows that the movement has been significant, particularly to Gauteng Province. Census 2001 shows that 20 per cent of the population was born outside the province. Studies based on the annual October Household Survey of Statistics South Africa show, however, that the end of apartheid has certainly not put an end to internal circular migration. Migration remains a major livelihoods strategy of most rural households. Fully 25 per cent of all households nationwide contain migrant workers. The proportion rises to over 40 per cent of households in deep rural areas. Johannesburg accounts for nearly 25 per cent of migrant destinations, followed by Pretoria (10 per cent), Durban (6 per cent) and Cape Town (4 per cent).

4.6.2 Importance of Migration to the Poor

South Africans, by and large, are internal migrants and do not migrate out of the country to the region (except as short-term visitors, tourists, for business, etc.). The question of the importance of migration to the poor therefore has two dimensions: does the presence of unskilled and semi-skilled migrants from other countries create fewer opportunities and greater impoverishment for South Africans? And second, has internal migration on the scale witnessed since the collapse of apartheid assisted households to deal with the appalling human legacy of that iniquitous system?

On the first question, for the South African government, every job occupied by a foreign migrant is potentially one less job for a population with formal unemployment rates of 30-40 per cent. The problem, as SAMP has demonstrated, is that although South Africans feel they are impoverished by the presence of non-South Africans, there is no hard evidence to support this belief. Very few say that they have ever lost a job to a foreigner and some studies suggest that some categories of migrant actually increase the size of the cake for South Africans by creating employment.

On the second question, the consensus seems to be that post-apartheid urbanization has simply displaced poverty from the countryside to the town. The growth of informal settlements in most major South African cities and towns is clear evidence of that position. The settlements are, of course, hives of informal sector activity which suggest that for some at least, the consequences of rapid urbanization may be facilitating a slow ascent out of absolute poverty.

4.6.3 International Migration and Brain Drain

The brain drain is a major issue of public and official concern within South Africa. Official emigration statistics clearly undercount the extent of the loss. Official data shows that 82,811 people emigrated from South Africa between 1989 and 1997. Official statistics from the 'big five' destination countries (Australia, Canada, New Zealand, UK, USA) show that 233,609 South Africans landed as immigrants over the same time period. For professionals, the comparable figures are 7,534 individuals (South Africa) and 19,890 (overseas).

Destination country statistics show 23,400 health workers from South Africa in the 'big five'. The OECD notes that this is equivalent to 10 per cent of all health professionals registered in the country, 'suggesting that emigration rates are significantly higher for health workers than skilled workers in general'.[308] Of these, 8,921 are practitioners, 6,844 nurses, and 7,642 other health professions. Some 3,146 South African nurses registered with the UK CC between 1998 and 2001.[309] In the United Kingdom, the OECD also estimates that 6 per cent of the total health workforce is South African.[310] The net training loss to South Africa is estimated at US$1 billion.

South Africa's Health Professionals Recruitment and Retention Strategy attempts to develop a broad-based and multi-faceted set of interventions, which includes addressing social and economic push factors.[311] Ironically, this strategy cannot address a major cause of emigration (crime and personal insecurity). And it makes no comment on the desirability of developing a strategy for replacement immigration. Restrictions on outward movement are not generally feasible in states that guarantee freedom of movement to citizens. Instead, Southern African states have also sought to exercise leverage over the pull factors by (ineffectual) appeals to the morality of industrial countries or

---

Box 17: Deportations and development

The collapse of the apartheid system in 1994 brought with it hopes of a new era of racial tolerance in South Africa. A decade later South Africa still remains deeply divided on racial, economic and social lines. On one thing virtually all South Africans agree, however: immigration is bad for the country and migrants, particularly from the rest of Africa, should be ostracised and shunned. Over one million irregular migrants have been deported from South Africa since 1994 and the methods used to identify and deport migrants are regularly criticised by South African and international human rights organizations. Most of those who are deported are unskilled and semi-skilled but are also engaged in some form of productive economic activity. Their households in neighbouring countries are heavily dependent on remittances and goods sent home by these migrants. While arrest and deportation of irregular migrants is uncontroversial as a policy tool, there is considerable doubt as to whether it is a cost-effective strategy for the state. Who it seems to enrich are those who administer the tough laws (reports of bribery and corruption are legion). There is also the distinct possibility that the disruption and cost of deportation have a profoundly disruptive effect on the migrants and their livelihoods.

Source: Klaaren and Ramji (2002); see endnote 287.

entering into bilateral or multilateral agreements with Western governments to control recruiting or hiring of professionals on a sectoral basis. The effectiveness of such agreements has yet to be properly tested.

A SAMP survey of 200 South African public and private sector enterprises in 1999 found only 2,000-3,000 foreign skilled personnel in total. The enterprises were asked to assess the impact of the brain drain on their operations. One third rated the outflow and impact of post-apartheid migration as 'significant'. On the other hand, 41 per cent said that the brain drain was of 'no importance' to their operations with another 26 per cent saying the impact was negligible. What this suggests is that at present there is no crippling shortage of skills across the board. Responses were sharply differentiated by sector. This suggests that brain drain impacts are likely to be sector and even firm-specific. A recent study of South Africa's R & D sector also found little concrete evidence of a 'brain drain crisis' in the private sector.[312] The actual labour market impacts of the brain drain have yet to be satisfactorily understood. These studies also provide insights into the reasons for the brain drain by asking respondents about factors that would promote or stop emigration. In general, push factors are much more important than pull factors in predisposing people to leave.

Little information exists on the remittance behaviour of South Africans who leave or the linkages maintained by the diaspora. In the last year, the South African media has been profiling what it calls the 'brain gain' of returning South Africans. There is little concrete evidence, however, that this return is either large or sustainable. The only attempt to tap the diaspora to date is the SANSA project, set up by the University of Cape Town and taken over by the National Research Foundation.[313] SANSA was designed to match diasporic South Africans with local employers for short-term assignments and employment. The intention was never to encourage permanent return. The success of this initiative is unknown.

4.6.4 Migration Policies

The migration issue has been central to the post-apartheid government's policy agenda. Regrettably, the development of a coherent and sound policy has been continuously compromised by political disagreement between the IFP (responsible for the immigration portfolio) and the ANC. The result was a painfully slow progression towards a post-apartheid immigration framework. A new Refugee Act (South Africa's first) took four years to craft; a new Immigration

Act (to replace the Aliens Control Act of 1991) nearly ten.

In the inter-regnum the anti-poor policies of the apartheid era Aliens Control Act continued to be enforced. The new Act is an improvement on the Aliens Control Act but does not promise a great deal for the poor. For example, the Act advocates a new openness towards immigration and puts new mechanisms in place to facilitate this process. In practice, the emphasis of the Act is almost exclusively on the highly skilled. It promises nothing to the unskilled or semi-skilled, and their South African employers, except tougher enforcement and increased xenophobia at the community level. The drafters of the Act also ignored the lobby that argued for a greater openness towards informal trade, a recommendation that would have had considerable implications for small entrepreneurs and the poor.

In many ways, the Act will simply entrench the status quo. By failing to provide reasonable means of controlled access to the South African labour market, the Act will drive labour migration further underground where exploitation and corruption already flourish. The effectiveness of mass deportations has already been called into question. The Act ensures that they will continue with a vengeance.

Only the mining industry escapes the Act's blandishments, again, an entrenchment of the status quo. Although the cost details are still being negotiated between Mozambique and South Africa, there is every indication that the mines will continue to enjoy unfettered access to foreign migrant labour. Access to such labour is governed by bilateral agreements signed in the 1970s and 1980s (between South Africa and Botswana, Lesotho, Mozambique and Swaziland). These agreements are badly outdated. When devised they did put in place basic protections for migrant workers but most of these are now redundant. These agreements badly need to be revisited and revised to take account of contemporary realities and to ensure that the benefits of migration continue to accrue to migrants and migrant households. One of the main unresolved issues is the compulsory deferred pay question (by which miners from Lesotho and Mozambique are forced to defer a portion of their wages back home). This system is opposed by miners and favoured by their dependents.

There are a number of key migration-related issues confronting South Africa. The first are the social, economic and fiscal implications of inter-provincial and rural-urban migration. These implications drive to questions of employment creation, resource allocation and urban governance. Some provincial and local authorities have begun to take the migration issue more seriously in the last three years. Both Gauteng Province and the Johannesburg City Council, for example, have commissioned SAMP to examine the implications of continued in-migration over the next 20 years.

Second, even in a country with a sophisticated infrastructure for data collection, migration policy decisions are made in an information vacuum. This is particularly evident in the assumptions underlying the White Paper on International Migration and the attendant Immigration Act. Both Statistics South Africa and Home Affairs have begun to investigate means of building internal capacity for the collection, analysis and use of migration data as a policymaking tool.

Third, the issue of good migration governance at the national level is critical. The Department of Home Affairs is under-resourced and, in the words of a former Director General, in a state of disrepair. The Home Affairs Turnaround Strategy, if implemented, promises a major shift towards good migration management through increased resourcing, capacity-building and the creation of a professional, client-oriented service.

The one issue that South Africa has sought most systematically to address in policy terms is the brain drain through high-profile involvement in multilateral initiatives and bilateral agreements with particular countries and sectors. The main thrust of these initiatives is to discourage 'recruiting' or 'poaching' of South Africans in South Africa. Another finding is that state efforts to restrict the brain drain through bonding or compulsory national service are likely to precipitate rather than slow emigration. Research on South Africa's compulsory community service programme for new health sector professionals shows widespread satisfaction with the system and a high propensity to emigrate (20-40 per cent) once the service is over.[314] Recent legislative moves to reform the public health sector in South Africa have received a less-than-enthusiastic response from doctors.

South Africa's dated bilateral labour treaties with Mozambique, Lesotho, Botswana and Swaziland urgently need to be revisited and updated or abolished. The unresolved question is whether the mining industry should still enjoy unfettered access to foreign labour and no obligation to employ South Africans, as it has in the past. The industry is pushing strongly for this 'right'. It is certain that other employers, without the economic organization and clout, will be unable to do the same.

South Africa's new Immigration Act should ensure that future policy gaps are around questions of implementation. In practice, the Act raises as many questions as it answers and has little concrete to offer on many key issues (informal trade, xenophobia). Even the role of an independent Immigration Advisory Board in developing policy is uncertain.

4.7 Malawi[315]

4.7.1 Introduction

Like other countries in the region, Malawi's migration regime has changed considerably over the last decade. In this case, Malawi has shifted from status as a classic 'labour reserve' to greatly reduced dependence on out-migration. This process was facilitated by the first inter-state disagreement in the region over HIV/AIDS policy.

After World War II, Malawi became the most important supplier of mine labour to South Africa. By the early 1970s, close to 120,000 Malawians worked on the South African mines. Malawians also migrated informally to work on commercial farms in Zimbabwe and South Africa and in South Africa's service sector. The majority of this migration was goal-directed. The model of a successful migrant career was to accumulate sufficient rural resources to invest in business activity at home and opt out of the system. Migrants from areas adjacent to the lake were particularly effective in using remittances to set themselves up in small business in the fishing industry.

In 1972, then-President Banda ordered the return of all Malawi's migrant miners from South Africa. Within a year, all had returned home. The option of using migration as a form of rural development was removed at a stroke. However, most returnees were absorbed into the commercial farming sector.

By the late 1970s, 15,000-20,000 Malawians were back on the mines. Then, in 1987, Banda ordered them to return when South Africa insisted on compulsory HIV/AIDS testing for all recruits. Mine migrancy therefore plays no role in contemporary Malawi, although the government has appealed to the South African mining industry on several occasions to take migrants back.

The majority of current migration out of the country for work is clandestine. The numbers are unknown but certainly do not compare with those from Mozambique. Even less is known, therefore, about remittance transfers and the potential role of remittances as a development resource in the country.

The other significant change for Malawi in the last decade has been the repatriation of several hundred thousand migrants from the south of the country to Mozambique. In March 1993, the Mozambican refugee population in Malawi was recorded at 1,057,314. This was about 10-12 per cent of the country's de jure population. In at least one district, Nsanje, at the southern end of the country, the refugee population was larger than the local population. Repatriation has certainly reduced the pressure on local communities and resources in the areas around the resettlement camps.

With little more than 10 per cent of Malawi's estimated 10.5 million people living in urban areas, the country is still predominantly rural. The largest urban centres in the country are Blantyre (including Limbe) and Zomba in the south, Lilongwe in the centre and Mzuzu in the north, which accommodate approximately 75 per cent of the national urban population. However, with high natural growth rates and increasing rural-urban migration, levels of urbanisation are rising in Malawi.

4.7.2 Importance of Migration to the Poor

Studies show that the transfer of cash incomes from urban workers to their rural homes is significant in Malawi, either in the form of investments or as family support. The 1998 Integrated Household Survey found that 13 per cent of rural households' cash income was from wage work. Migrants within Malawi, and beyond the country's borders, behave like typical 'target workers', earning cash incomes in towns and repatriating these and investing them in micro-enterprises in the rural villages. Urban wage incomes thus bolster rural economic enterprises. Another common way is through the purchase of farm inputs, including fertilisers and seeds. Almost every rural household in Malawi depends on family members working in towns for its farm inputs. Through this practice the urban workers are in turn able to maintain ties with their rural places of origin.

A recent study observed that rural dependence on off-farm income (from urban areas) and from out-migration in general has a number of implications for rural socio-economic structures. These include the relief of pressure on land, increased influx of money into the rural economy, investments in agricultural production and small-scale enterprises, investments in rural transportation (mini-buses, trucks and push bikes) and hence ease of access to commodity markets, and improvements in rural housing.

Another very important linkage, but particularly difficult to quantify, is trade between the rural and urban areas. The dependence on off-farm incomes for the majority of the rural households results in the emergence of a wide range of commercial activities between rural and urban communities. There are a large number of rotating markets that facilitate the circulation of goods and cash. A common feature at these markets is the itinerant traders that operate across district, regional, and, in some cases, international borders.

Many of the goods traded are thus brought in from outside the areas of the markets – often from towns and beyond political boundaries, with the latter being especially important in border districts. The existence of long, open, and poorly policed borders between Malawi and its immediate neighbours facilitates the unhindered movement of traders and their goods.

4.7.3 Migration Policy

Malawian immigration policy is similar to that of other countries in its focus on enforcement rather than proactive recruitment of immigrants.

The country is still dealing with the Banda legacy of enforced cessation of legal migration to South Africa in the 1970s and 1980s. Mine migrancy is no longer a strategy for household income-generation, although the South Africa-Malawi bilateral agreement has never been officially rescinded.

Most Malawian migrants now leave the country as undocumented migrants with all of the difficulties and vulnerabilities associated with that status. Malawi would clearly benefit from the freeing up of movement within the SADC region.

Malawi's PRSP has been widely praised for its relevance and comprehensive character. Like many other PRSPs it does, at least, acknowledge the importance of migrant remittances to rural poverty reduction. However, the issue is largely forgotten when it comes to policy recommendations. As in other countries, migration realities need to be mainstreamed into government policy reduction policies.

4.8 Mozambique

4.8.1 Introduction

Migration is one of the mainstays of the Mozambican economy and plays a critical role in securing a livelihood for tens of thousands of Mozambican households. Migration has recently been described as the 'lifeblood' of southern Mozambique. An estimated 500,000 Mozambican migrants work outside the country, more than in any domestic sector of the Mozambican economy. Approximately 80,000 of these migrants are legally employed in the South

African mining industry; the rest work in commercial agriculture, manufacturing, the services industry and in the informal sector. Mozambicans also cross borders to work in Zimbabwe and Swaziland.

Since 1990, and the end of apartheid and Mozambique's civil war, established patterns of cross-border and internal migration have intensified and altered in various ways. Mozambique, for example, is now the single largest supplier of mine labour to South Africa. Annual remittances through formal channels total US $32 million. Informal remittances and remittances 'in kind' mean that the 'value package' is a major contributor to Mozambican livelihoods and the country's foreign exchange earnings.

Another increasingly important form of mobility between South Africa and its neighbours is informal cross-border trade. Women are perhaps the primary participants and beneficiaries of such movement. The dimensions of trade are unknown because much of it is currently 'clandestine' in the sense that there are no formal structures for monitoring trade and many overt and hidden obstacles for the trader. Nevertheless, cross-border trade is becoming a major income-generating strategy for urban and rural households, particularly those with female heads. As the SADC region moves towards free trade by 2008, the obstacles to informal trade should be systematically reduced. Informal trade will then become an even greater opportunity for income generation, sustainable livelihoods and poverty reduction. Women would be the greatest beneficiaries.

One of the major features of post-war Mozambican migration to South Africa is its irregular or undocumented nature. The scale of undocumented migration is a function of the pull of the South African labour market for many Mozambicans. Migrants are vulnerable and exploited and enjoy few of the protections and rights of legal workers. Along with persistent violation of basic rights, migrants are seen as 'job-stealers', criminals and disease-carriers and become the objects of xenophobia.

Another factor affecting the extent to which Mozambique benefits from migration is the degree of permanence of migration. The repatriation of over 300,000 displaced Mozambicans in South Africa during the war did not take place as planned when they were offered permanent residence rights. Over 200,000 former refugees accepted this offer and have been integrated to varying degrees into South African communities. The extent to which these former refugees maintain contacts with home is uncertain.

A new phenomenon observed more recently is when Mozambican migrants maintain a household and dependents in South Africa and Mozambique simultaneously. This has considerable implications for Mozambican households dependent on migrant earnings. One counter-strategy has been for wives to move to South Africa to be with their spouses and reduce the likelihood of transnational households emerging. Clearly permanent emigration to South Africa is counterproductive for Mozambique. At the same time, to the extent that emigrants have incentives and avenues for maintaining contact, some of the benefits will still flow back across the border.

4.8.2 Importance of Migration to the Poor

Out-migration is clearly of great significance to the poor of Mozambique, both urban and rural. Any country that sends 500,000 migrants abroad every year is going to be heavily impacted by its ability to maximise the fruits of migration. Fortunately for Mozambique, the evidence suggests that most migrants see Mozambique as home and migrate in order to build wealth and security in Mozambique.

Clearly, migration throws up major developmental, policy and capacity-building challenges for a country such as Mozambique seeking to reduce poverty and inequality. At present, the influence of cross-border migration on economic and social development for Mozambique is poorly understood and definitely underestimated. Mozambique's CDPF is virtually silent on an issue that affects the lives and livelihoods of so many poor Mozambicans.

Through remittances especially, migration has the potential to contribute positively to economic development while the continued outflow of labour unskilled and skilled simultaneously can also destabilise this process. The lack of up-to-date information on migration and continued implementation of outdated immigration legislation pose additional barriers.

Out-migration is clearly geographically differentiated in Mozambique with the south of the country heavily integrated into regional migration streams, and the centre and north hardly at all. Recent work by de Vletter demonstrates that in relative terms, it is the south of the country that is much better off. The connection between migration and poverty alleviation seems to be relatively clear.

Informal trade with South Africa and Zimbabwe is another key area with implications for the poor, especially women. By freeing up informal trade with neighbouring countries, small-scale entrepreneurship (currently mired in red tape) would be able to grow and flourish.

4.8.3 Migration Policies

Contract migration to South Africa is governed by a bilateral agreement signed between South Africa and the Portuguese as long ago as 1964. The new South African Immigration Act threatens to impose a levy on all Mozambicans employed legally in South Africa. The two governments are currently discussing an exemption for Mozambicans. In fact, the whole agreement needs to be reviewed and revised, so outdated are most of its provisions.

Mozambique has a vested interest in maximising the flow of migrants to the South African mines. Mozambique has been the only country to increase its market share over the last decade. The reasons have more to do with mine politics than national policy, particularly the lack of militancy of Mozambican workers.

The whole remittance system to Mozambique needs further study and encouragement. One contentious policy area is that of deferred pay. Mozambican miners are forced to compulsorily defer up to 60 per cent of their pay. This policy is opposed by miners. However, SAMP research shows that it

---

Box 18: Maintaining mine labour from Mozambique

Mozambique has supplied migrant contract workers to the South African gold mines for over a century. Mozambican society, particularly in the South, has been profoundly shaped by generations of migration. Since the late 1980s, the South African gold mining industry has been in a prolonged state of crisis with mine closures and major retrenchments. The mine workforce has been cut in half since 1987 from over 400,000 to under 200,000. Every internal and external migrant sending area has been extremely hard hit by retrenchments which have exacerbated household poverty and raised unemployment levels. All, that is, except Mozambique. The number of miners from Mozambique has remained virtually the same for the last two decades. The proportion of Mozambican migrants in the mine workforce increased from 10 per cent to over 25 per cent. The mines retain control over where they get their labour so this is a deliberate choice on their part. Why this loyalty to the Mozambican miner? Some say that it is because Mozambican workers are less militant, more compliant and accepting of poorer working conditions. The reasons for that lie not in any cultural predisposition to complacency but the vulnerability of workers from poverty-stricken areas with little choice. They would rather work on the mines than not work at all.

Source: Crush and Tshitereke (2002); see endnote 289.

is favoured by miners' dependents. In other words, while deferred pay appears to violate the rights of the miner it does bring benefit to households who have a greater chance of accessing it.

Detailed and up-to-date data on migrants and immigrants would allow Mozambique to deal more effectively with the challenge of integrating migration into poverty reduction strategies. It would also allow the country to establish new national approaches and policies on migration that can play a larger part in pro-poor growth and social development.

By producing a comprehensive, reliable knowledge base on migration and local capacity to manage and advise on migration challenges, flows of people and remittances could be channelled more effectively towards productive investment and sustained economic growth.

The South African deportation system is riddled with abuse and corruption and is increasingly recognised as completely ineffectual. Trafficking of migrants and women and children for sexual exploitation is also on the increase, further victimising the vulnerable migrant. Both governments will need to eventually come to terms with the inevitability of Mozambican migration and transform its management into an orderly and workable system as part of a joint commitment to the good governance of migration. Mozambique needs to develop greater capacity to advocate for the rights of migrants, develop workable models of migration regulation and to effectively manage the movement of people across borders in the interests of migrants. Only then will the material benefits of migration accrue to Mozambique rather than the South African police and border guards involved in the corruption industry.

Mozambique, like all of the countries in Southern Africa, is currently being ravaged by the HIV/AIDS epidemic. The epidemic will exact a major toll on the national economy as well as the livelihoods of individual households and communities through its impact on rural agricultural production. The particular intersection of migration and HIV/AIDS is being increasingly recognised by governments. Migration plays a major role in the dissemination of the virus to rural areas in Mozambique. Migrants have also been shown to be particularly vulnerable to infection. Conventional interventions to prevent infection and control the spread of HIV/AIDS are generally ineffectual amongst migrants and in migrant communities. Information on migration patterns and sexual networking could play a significant role in the development of workable interventions and thereby contain the spread of the disease.

4.9 Zambia

4.9.1 Introduction

Zambia's national migration regime is distinctive from that of the other countries reviewed in this volume. Historically, Zambia received migrants from Malawi and Congo to work on the country's copper mines. The mine workforce was stabilised and internalised several decades ago.

Zambia is neither a country of significant out-migration nor in-migration of the poor. Foreign migrants comprised only 1 per cent of the population in 2000 (down from 4 per cent in 1980). In absolute terms, there were 328,188 foreign-born people in Zambia in 1969. This number had fallen to 92,504 in 2000.

The country has experienced a brain drain of professionals over the last decade, but this has not been as voluminous or serious in its consequences as that from Zimbabwe or South Africa. Systematic information on the extent of the brain drain is unavailable. As an example, one study estimates that only 50 of 600 doctors trained in Zambia since independence remain in the public health service.[316]

Cross-border trading is the primary income generating form of migration for Zambia's poor. The country has an extremely active Cross Border Traders' Association that advocates for reforms and advances the interests of its members with national governments and regional bodies such as COMESA.

Internal migration is the primary form of migration affecting the poor in Zambia. The country is one of the most urbanised states in the region with a significant permanent urban population. Census data shows that the proportion of the population defined as migrant declined from 22 per cent in 1980 to 18 per cent in 2000. The number of people captured as migrants increased from 1.18 million in 1969 to 1.68 million in 2000. Rural-urban links are weaker in Zambia than in any other country, with the possible exception of South Africa.

During the 1990s, Zambia experienced a mass influx of refugees from the civil war in Angola. Estimates are in the 250,000-300,000 range. Refugee camps were established and there was limited integration of refugees into mainstream Zambian society. With the end of the civil war, voluntary repatriation is currently under way.

4.9.2 Importance of Migration to the Poor

In the past, urban-rural links were strong in Zambia and migration played a major role in rural household strategies for survival. Divided households are still common but it is extremely difficult for poor urban dwellers to access the resources and remittances to support rural families.

One study of southern Zambia suggested that the primary determinant of out-migration was lack of access to land and productive resources. On the other hand, with the harsh economic conditions in Zambian cities, regular 'remittances' do not exist. In fact, sending gifts or assistance to family back in the village is almost non existent'.[317]

One consequence of urban poverty and unemployment has been a process of de-urbanization with unemployed urban dwellers re-migrating back to the countryside on a permanent basis to support themselves on the land. Urban Zambia experienced net out-migration between 1990 and 2000, and rural Zambia net in-migration. The Copperbelt districts experienced the highest rates of outmigration (137 per thousand). The questions raised by this tendency need further examination, since they may prefigure a broader regional trend.

4.9.3 Migration Policies

Like other countries in the region, Zambia does not have a proactive immigration policy. The foreign-born population of the country has actually declined significantly over the last three decades. The thrust of policy focuses on exclusion and control.

Zambia's unique internal and external migration history requires further study. The fact that Zambia is one of the most urbanised countries in the region has made the challenge of urban poverty reduction particularly important. This fact is well-recognised in the country's PRSP.

The PRSP dubiously asserts that the urban and rural populations are disconnected and that there is no significant pattern of remittances back to the rural areas. This issue needs further examination. So too does the question of de-urbanization and its implications for poverty in both urban and rural Zambia.

The particular needs of cross-border traders, vis-à-vis restrictive cross-border travel to neighbouring countries needs to be addressed, given Zambia's role in both COMESA and the SADC.

As in other countries, migration is not factored into the country's PRSP. In the Zambian case, unlike elsewhere, it might be argued that this omission is justified in light of the relative unimportance of migration as a poverty response and alleviator. However, the government's policy still needs to be re-examined to ensure that it is not overlooking hidden potentials and impacts of migration, particularly de-urbanization.

4.10 Zimbabwe

4.10.1 Introduction

Zimbabwe is in the unusual historical position of being both a labour importer, exporter and corridor, the precise balance of roles varying over time. During the colonial period, Zimbabwe's mines and commercial farms attracted migrants from countries such as Malawi, Mozambique and Zambia. South Africa, in turn, attracted unskilled and semi-skilled Zimbabweans to its own farms and mines.

The 1992 Census showed that of the 10.4 million people in the country, 453,405 (4.4 per cent) were born outside Zimbabwe including 165,000 Mozambicans, 38,000 Malawians and 10,000 Zambians. The 2002 Census indicates a significant decline in the number of Mozambicans (returning home after the war).

Since independence, Zimbabwe has experienced a number of shifts in traditional migration patterns. Some are the result of general social and economic change in the region. Others are a very direct result of Zimbabwe's economic decline and political malaise. Notable are the following:

- Zimbabwe is no longer a significant recipient of migrant labour except, perhaps, on the border with Mozambique.

- The Mugabe government's land policy has left significant numbers of first- and second-generation migrant farmworkers without economic support. Indeed, it has been suggested that farmworkers on commercial farms have been the major victims of the policy.

- The volume of cross-border traffic between Zimbabwe and its neighbours has escalated dramatically over the last decade as job opportunities within the country have shrunk. In the main, these are moves of the poor and impoverished.

- Migration prompted by the search for a livelihood has increased dramatically in the last five years. South Africa and Botswana have been the major destinations. Both have reacted by deporting undocumented migrants in growing numbers (about 90,000 per annum from South Africa at the present time).

- Informal trade between South Africa and Zimbabwe has mushroomed since 1994. This trade, in which women are significant players, has been studied in some depth. South Africa's current restrictions on movement from Zimbabwe are causing major difficulties for small traders. Zimbabwean women also trade extensively with countries to the north (Malawi, Zambia, Tanzania).

- Internal rural-urban migration increased dramatically after independence. The colonial pattern of circulation has increasingly been replaced by a more stable urban population. Many first-generation migrants retain strong links with the rural home but linkages are loosening with the second generation.

The most dramatic development of the last decade has been a massive bleed of skills from a once-vibrant economy. Zimbabwe's brain drain has assumed crisis proportions and shows no signs of decelerating. One recent study notes the difficulty of obtaining brain drain statistics that are 'accurate, reliable, comparable and detailed'.[318] At the same time, a seemingly precise figure of 479,348 Zimbabweans has been advanced as the total number of Zimbabweans outside the country, including 176,400 in the UK, 165,375 in Botswana, 33,075 in the USA and 22,050 in South Africa.

The source of these figures is unclear, as are the findings reported from a survey of diasporic Zimbabweans.[319] A SAMP survey of a representative sample of skilled Zimbabweans in 2001 showed that the brain drain is likely to accelerate in the foreseeable future. There, 27 per cent of skilled respondents were committed to emigrating within 6 months, 55 per cent within 2 years and 67 per cent within 5 years. Conventional economic push factors were seen as most important: taxes, cost of living and public services. In the case of the health sector, the Ministry of Health does not have precise figures because departing health professionals are 'not willing to announce their destinations' and many who leave choose to keep their registration active'.[320]

Statistics are anecdotal at best: for example, of 1,200 physicians trained in Zimbabwe in the 1990s, only 360 were left in 2001, or that Zambia has retained only 50 of more than 600 doctors trained since independence.[321] Clearly a far more detailed inventory is needed than currently exists. In

Box 19: The Zimbabwean diaspora

The political and economic crisis in Zimbabwe has prompted a major exodus of skills to other countries in the region and overseas. The UK and South Africa have been major beneficiaries of this brain drain. The health sector has been particularly hard-hit. Unless there is an economic turnaround in the country, this skills flight is likely to continue, making life still harder for those who remain. Ironically, the Zimbabwean economy is now increasingly propped up by those who have left. Zimbabwe's diaspora retains a keen interest in their country and sends large sums of money home to relatives who remain. The government has sought to gain greater control over the remittance flow and has also established a programme called Homelink which is designed to encourage diasporic Zimbabweans to remit through formal channels, to purchase property and to invest in the country. Homelink is a subsidiary of the Reserve Bank of Zimbabwe and remains deeply controversial within the diaspora.

Source: www.homelinkzimbabwe.com

Zimbabwe, a new initiative to resettle and reintegrate diasporic Zimbabweans is underway. However, without a significant change in the circumstances that are forcing Zimbabweans to leave it is hard to see such an initiative having much short-term success, much less compensate for the ongoing brain drain.

Internal migration, and accompanying accelerated urbanization, has been a notable feature of Zimbabwe's human landscape in the last two decades. This process has been studied in some detail, and the enduring character of rural-urban migration established.[322] Studies of remittance behaviour of migrants have broader implications for poverty reduction more generally. Work on remittances had shown (a) that 25 per cent of rural household income comes from remittances; (b) that remittances play a significant role in raising agricultural productivity; (c) that households with access to remittances are more able to invest in agricultural inputs; (d) that the dependence of rural households on income coming from migrants is higher in the drier regions of the country and (e) that remittance flows have declined in the 1990s consequent upon growing urban unemployment.[323] One study has suggested that rural households are now sending 'reverse remittances' to support urban households.

4.10.2 Importance of Migration to the Poor

In Zimbabwe's current straitened circumstances, migration has become a key response of both the poor and the better-off. The large numbers of migrants now heading south are doing so in direct response to the situation in Zimbabwe and the perception of economic opportunity in South Africa and Botswana. The problem is that their reception has been frosty, to say the least. This is pushing migrants into low-wage jobs with few rights and protections. The case of commercial farms along the South Africa-Zimbabwe border has been studied. Conditions on the farms are particularly exploitative as farmers take advantage of the presence of Zimbabwean migrants.

As a result, the possible benefits of migration to Zimbabwe are not being maximised. Not only are migrants themselves being exploited but they are not in a position to remit the kinds of funds that their households desperately need.

The poor are also incidental victims of the brain drain. The brain drain has been particularly significant in the public health sector. Seriously short-staffed and under-resourced, the health sector is in crisis and simply unable to meet the basic health needs of the Zimbabwean population, a significant deterioration from the situation a decade ago when universal access to primary health care was Zimbabwe's great post-independence achievement.

Internally, it is clear that households in drier and more marginal areas of the country are likely to be more dependent on remittances. Interruptions in the flow of remittances as a result of urban unemployment are therefore likely to lead to greater impoverishment in the poorer parts of the country.

At this time of economic stress, informal cross-border trading has assumed increased importance as a livelihoods strategy. Muzvidizwa shows that urban households in Masvingo have used trading as a successful strategy for climbing out of poverty.[324]

4.10.3 Migration Policies

Like most countries in SADC, Zimbabwe has not encouraged permanent immigration since independence. Issues of immigration and citizenship are governed by three principal pieces of legislation: the Immigration Act, the Refugees Act and the Citizenship of Zimbabwe Act. The Immigration Act empowers the Minister of Home Affairs to determine who may enter the country and under what conditions. Persons wishing to come to Zimbabwe for work are admitted only if prospective employers can demonstrate to the Foreign Recruitment Committee that the skills are unavailable locally. Temporary residence for periods of up to five years is generally all that is permitted.

Zimbabwe is probably the firmest supporter of the SADC Draft Migration Protocol. This is unsurprising. With burgeoning unemployment and an increasingly important role as a migrant exporter, Zimbabwe would benefit considerably from more open borders across the region.

The Zimbabwean government has expressed recurrent concern about the brain drain and has contemplated measures to discourage professionals from leaving. However, only fundamental attention to the structural conditions encouraging the skilled to leave would likely make any difference. The solution is to be found in political and economic reform, not ad hoc migration policy measures.

The fundamental policy challenge in Zimbabwe is to decipher whether the extraordinary migration movements out of the country in the last decade are a temporary aberration or prefigure a more permanent way of life for Zimbabweans. Levels of dissatisfaction are so high that barring fundamental economic and political reform, out-migration will continue and even accelerate. While this may have positive benefits for those left behind, in the form of remittance flows primarily, the current situation is ultimately unsustainable.

Anecdotal evidence suggests that diasporic Zimbabweans maintain strong linkages with home and that most see emigration as a temporary phenomenon or response. A study by the National Economic Consultative Forum argued that the Zimbabwe diaspora was 'unique' in the strength of the 'organic links' with home of 480,000 professionals living overseas. Some 70 per cent of those interviewed expressed a 'strong desire' to return home. However, the longer that perceived conditions in the country continue to deteriorate, the more likely it is that they will become progressively more integrated into host societies. Certainly second-generation emigrants will be less and less inclined to return.

Patterns of out-migration and informal cross-border trade can be seen as a direct survival strategy by poor households. Migration in Zimbabwe, then, is a direct response to poverty. Whether migration, particularly of the clandestine kind, gives the participants and their dependents full value is probably doubtful. In other words, migration is a poverty alleviation but not poverty reduction strategy.

The policy challenge that will face any future government is how to reverse the tide of out-migration and provide economic and other incentives for diasporic Zimbabweans to return or maintain strong linkages with home.

Appendix 1 Mean annual flows to Europe and US, 1995-2000				
	To Europe (1)	USA (2)	Total (Europe and USA)	Population (3)	Av annual emigration rate 1995-2000 %
East Africa					
Somalia	5949	2744	8693	8,175,320	0.11
Ethiopia	2749	5081	7831	61,266,000	0.01
Kenya	2336	1632	3968	28,726,000	0.01
Eritrea	770	686	1457	3,879,000	0.04
Tanzania	759	435	1194	32,128,480	0.00
Uganda	710	372	1082	21,040,000	0.01
Rwanda	744	92	836	7,284,000	0.01
Burundi	326	36	362	6,548,190	0.01
Djibouti	42	16	59	608,150	0.01
Total East Africa	14385	11095	25481	169,655,140	0.02
Central Africa					
Congo, Dem Rep	4175	262	4437	48,178,170	0.01
Cameroon	2120	765	2885	14,238,860	0.02
Congo, Rep	1067	94	1161	2,850,060	0.04
Equatorial Guinea	538	3	541	433,060	0.12
Sao Tome	233	5	238	141,700	0.17
Gabon	117	18	136	1,167,290	0.01
CAR	93	9	102	3,603,400	0.00
Chad	56	16	72	7,282,870	0.00
Total Central Africa	8400	1171	9571	77,895,410	0.01
West Africa					
Nigeria	7204	7736	14940	120,817,300	0.01
Ghana	5840	4563	10403	18,449,370	0.06
Senegal	4894	480	5374	9,033,530	0.06
Cape Verde	2514	951	3465	412,240	0.84
Sudan	1386	1650	3036	29,978,890	0.01
Liberia	981	1817	2798	2,961,520	0.09
Cote d'Ivoire	2046	377	2423	15,159,110	0.02
Sierra Leone	910	1374	2284	4,830,480	0.05

Togo	1155	225	1380	4,258,140	0.03
Mali	1258	97	1354	10,333,640	0.01
Gambia, The	1008	196	1204	1,223,810	0.10
Guinea	965	98	1063	7,086,120	0.01
Guinea-Bissau	884	89	973	1,149,330	0.08
Mauritania	583	48	631	2,493,120	0.03
Burkina Faso	528	21	549	10,730,330	0.01
Niger	180	212	392	10,125,740	0.00
Benin	306	46	353	5,950,330	0.01
Western Sahara	1	1	2	-	-
Total West Africa	32642	19980	52622	254,993,000	0.02
Southern Africa					
South Africa	10825	2323	13148	41,402,390	0.03
Mauritius	2700	54	2754	1,159,730	0.24
Angola	2056	82	2138	12,401,580	0.02
Zimbabwe	1653	275	1928	12,153,850	0.02
Zambia	584	213	796	9,665,710	0.01
Namibia	607	26	633	1,681,820	0.04
Madagascar	584	37	621	14,592,380	0.00
Malawi	514	55	569	9,884,000	0.01
Comoros	290	2	291	530,820	0.05
Mozambique	221	45	266	16,965,000	0.00
Botswana	208	14	222	1,614,190	0.01
Seychelles	52	14	66	78,850	0.08
Swaziland	18	13	31	990,530	0.00
Lesotho	15	8	22	1,978,090	0.00
Others	59	-	-	-	-
Total Southern Africa	20385	3158	23484	125,098,940	0.02
Africa - Others	8413	-	-	-	-
Total Africa	84226	35404	111157	627,642,490	0.02

Notes: (1) Immigration of Africa citizens to European countries, by citizenship, 1995-2001, Copyright Eurostat. All Rights Reserved.
(2) US immigrants admitted by region and country of birth fiscal years 1995-2001, 2002 Year Book of Immigration Statistics,
U.S. Department of Homeland Security, Office of Immigration Statistics 2003.
(3) Population Estimate 1998, World Development Indicators Data Query Service: http://devdata.world-bank.org/data-query/

Appendix 2: Availability of data on internal migration				
Countries	Last census	Next census	Census includes internal migration data?	Internal migration survey
East Africa				
Somalia	1987	2003	No	No
Ethiopia	1994	2004	Yes	1999 Labour Force Survey
Kenya	1999	2009	Yes	No
Eritrea	1984	2003	Yes	No
Tanzania	2002		No	No
Uganda	2002		Yes	No
Rwanda	2002		Yes	No
Burundi	1990		No	No
Djibouti	1983	2003	Yes	No
Central Africa				
Congo, DR				
Cameroon	1987	2003	Yes	No
Congo, Rep.				
Eq. Guinea	1994		No	No
Sao Tome	2001		No	No
Gabon	1993	2003	Yes	No
CAR	1988	2003	Yes	No
Chad	1993	2003	Yes	No
West Africa				
Nigeria	1991	2004	No	Survey of internal migration and tourism
Ghana	2000	2010	Yes	Migration Research Study in Ghana (1995)
Senegal	2002	2009	Yes	No
Cape Verde	2000	2010	Yes	No
Sudan	1993	2003	Yes	No
Liberia	1984	2003	Yes	No
Cote d'Ivoire				
Sierra Leone	1985	2003	Yes	No
Togo	1981		Yes	No

Mali	1998	2008	Yes	No
Gambia, The	1993	2003	Yes	No
Guinea	1996		Yes	No
Guinea-Bissau	1991		No	No
Mauritania	2000		Yes	No
Burkina Faso	1996	2006	Yes	No
Niger	2001		Yes	Survey of migration and urbanisation (1993)
Benin	2002		Yes	No
Western Sahara				
Southern Africa				
South Africa	2001	2006	Yes	University of Pretoria Project on Internal Migration
Mauritius	2000	2010	Yes	No
Angola	1970	2004	No	No
Zimbabwe	2002		Yes	No
Zambia	2000	2010	Yes	No
Namibia	2001	2011	Yes	Intercensal demographic survey
Madagascar	1993	2003	Yes	No
Malawi	1998	2008	No	No
Comoros	1991		No	No
Mozambique	1997		Yes	No
Botswana	2001	2011	Yes	No
Seychelles	2002		Yes	No
Swaziland	1997	2007	Yes	Demographic and Housing Survey
Lesotho	2001	2005	Yes	No

Source: Data compiled from website of Queensland Centre for Population Research, http://www.geosp.uq.edu.au/qcpr/database/IMdata/lmdata.htm

Appendix 3: Summary of PRSP comments on migration				
Country	Negative	Neutral	Positive	Policy
Benin	Emigration of children causes poverty	Movement from land scarce areas to land available areas		None
Burkina Faso	• Development inequalities cause migration • Internal and external migration exacerbate HIV/AIDS			• Incentives to prevent young people abandoning their land • Narrow development gaps between regions
Burundi	Displaced people depend on charity			Socio-economic reintegration of displaced prioritised
Cameroon				• ICTs to prevent rural outmigration • Train and recruit teachers to prevent migration to foreign universities • Limit outmigration by promoting income generating activities in rural areas
Cape Verde	• Restrictive measures in host countries have cut remittances • Rural-urban migration transfers problems to urban environment		• Emigration a social buffer • Emigration a survival strategy	• Promote remittances • Engage emigrants in implementing national development strategy • Develop ethnic markets abroad
DR Congo	Mass displacement a problem			Reunite families and relocate displaced communities

Côte d'Ivoire	• Domestic and foreign migration impoverishes the vulnerable • Immigration linked to soaring crime			
Djibouti	Urban migration caused by drought			Need study of effects of immigration
Ethiopia	Spontaneous migration causes NR degradation		Planned resettlement from highland to lowland can be beneficial	
Gambia	• Immigration leads to high population growth rates • Rural areas left underpopulated • New problems in urban areas • Economic downturn has reduced opportunities in urban areas without promoting return	Seasonal return during rainy months		
Ghana	Migration from north caused by poverty			
Guinea	Urban problems exacerbated by 'urban drift'			Aim to improve mobility through improved road network
Kenya	Migration breaks down traditional social protection			

Malawi	• Poverty of south partly caused by migration • Illegal immigration causes crime and undermines integrity of passports • Migration breaks down male-female relations • Male migration leaves illiterate women managing farms and families			
Mali			Emigration attenuates demographic growth	
Mauritania	• Drought and poor living conditions cause migration of poor • Urbanization creates shanty towns, environmental problems and pressure on services			Create viable jobs in urban areas
Mozambique	• Urbanization low, but rural-urban migration likely in future			
Niger	• Internal and external migration helps spread HIV/AIDS • Outmigration a cause of poverty		Migrant remittances an important source of household income	

Rwanda	Distress migration in some areas due to drought	The 'money rich' migrate	• Seasonal migration of labour a 'social mechanism' • Loss of outmigration options has negatively affected poor households	Priority to resettlement of the displaced
São Tomé and Principe	Poverty causes migration to cities			
Senegal			Emigrants can revitalise economic activities in rural areas through investment, advice and identification of niches for rural products	• Outreach to migrants • Incentives for emigrants to invest in rural production
Sierra Leone	Internal displacement disrupted agriculture, education, spread crime and HIV/ AIDS			Focus on improving living standards of displaced and returnees

Source: PRSP and IPRSP documents for each country, searched March 2004.
Note: The following countries did not mention migration in their PRSPs: CAR, Chad, Guinea-Bissau, Madagascar, Tanzania, Uganda, Zambia.

Notes

1   See http://www.africa-union.org/home/Welcome.htm

2   ILO, *ILO Activities in Africa, 2000-2003*. ILO Tenth African Regional Meeting, Addis Ababa, 2003, p. 41.

3   IOM, *World Migration Report 2003: Challenges and Responses for People on the Move* (Geneva: IOM. 2003).

4   H. Zlotnik, "International Migration, 1965-96" *Population and Development Review* 24 (1998): 429-86.

5   A. Adepoju, "Preliminary Analysis of Emigration Dynamics in Sub-Saharan Africa" *International Migration* 32 (1994): 197-216.

6   The major hosting nations in Africa are Tanzania, Uganda, Kenya, Sudan, Congo, Zambia and Guinea; see UNHCR, *Populations of Concern to UNHCR* (Geneva: UNHCR, 2003).

7   See Global IDP project website at http://www.idpproject.org/regions/Africa_idps.htm

8   There is also substantial migration to the Gulf, although accurate data on this is unavailable.

9   LSMS are available in Ghana for 1985, 1987, 1988, 1991 and 1998, for Tanzania in 1991 (Kagera region only) and 1993, South Africa for 1993, and Côte d'Ivoire annually for 1985-88. See http://www.worldbank.org/lsms/

10   According to IOM, *World Migration Report 2003*, half of Africa's migrants are women.

11   C. Tacoli, "Changing Rural-Urban Interactions in Sub-Saharan Africa and their Impacts on Livelihoods: A Summary" Report for International Institute for Environment and Development, London, 2002, p. 20.

12   ILO, "Decent Work for Africa's Development" Report of Director General to 10th Annual ILO Regional Meeting, Addis Ababa, 2003, p. 11

13   D. Potts, "Shall We Go Home? Increasing Urban Poverty in African Cities and Migration Processes" *Geographical Journal* 161(3) (2001): 245-64.

14   W. Carrington and E. Detragiache, "How Extensive Is the Brain Drain?" *Finance & Development* 36 (1999).

15   *Ibid.*

16   UN, *International Migration 2002 Wallchart*, UN Population Division, Department of Economic and Social Affairs, New York, 2003.

17   IOM, *World Migration Report 2003*, p. 223.

18   *Ibid.* It might be questioned whether these skilled expatriates are technically 'replacing' Africans who move abroad, or whether their employment reflects the broader structure of overseas aid that emphasises management by 'international' staff and the need for 'technical cooperation.'

19   A. Essy, "The Role of Higher Education Institutions in the Building of the African Union."

Conference of Rectors, Vice Chancellors and Presidents of African Universities, Grand Bay, Mauritius, March 2003.

20   L. Kupfer, K. Jarawan, J. Bridbord, J. McDermott and K. Hofman, *Strategies to Prevent Brain Drain* (Arusha: Global Forum for Health Research, 2002).

21   See http://www.africasbraingain.org

22   See http://www.africarecruit.com

23   C. Chikezie, "Supporting Africa's Regional Integration: The African Diaspora – Prototype Pan-Africanists or Parochial Village-Aiders." Report of African Knowledge Networks Forum (AKNF), Addis Ababa, October 2001.

24   See http://www.iom.int/MIDA/mida_health.shtml

25   The African Law Institute plans to establish a web-based African Legal Skills Bank. See http://www.africalawinstitute.org/talent.html

26   The MIDA programme partially replaces the Return of Qualified African Nations (RQAN) programme, which facilitated the return of only 2,500 professionals between 1983-99. Ongoing MIDA programmes focus on the Great Lakes, Somalia, Ghana and Guinea.

27   See http://www.africa-union.org

28   AU, "Resolution (Regulation) on Establishment of a Strategic Framework for a Policy of Migration in Africa" at *Ibid*.

29   See http://www.africalawinstitute.org/talent.html

30   Interview with Eric Buch, NEPAD Special Advisor on Health, 18 February 2004.

31   WHO, *Migration of Health Personnel: A Challenge for Health Systems in Africa* (Geneva, World Health Organisation, 2003).

32   B. Stilwell, K. Diallo, P. Zurn, M. Poz, O. Adams and J. Buchan, "Developing Evidence-Based Ethical Policies on the Migration of Health Workers: Conceptual and Practical Challenges" *Human Resources for Health* 1(1) (2003).

33   A number of countries worldwide have sought to restrict the entry of migrants with (or suspected of having) HIV/AIDS, whilst some countries have sought to deport migrant sex workers through fear of the epidemic spreading; see R. Parker and P. Aggleton, *HIV/AIDS-Related Stigma and Discrimination: A Conceptual Framework and Agenda for Action* (Washington DC: Horizons Program, The Population Council, 2002).

34   See J. Handmaker, L. de la Hunt and J. Klaaren, (eds.), *Perspectives on Refugee Protection in South Africa* (Pretoria: Lawyers for Human Rights, 2001).

35   Burkina Faso, Cape Verde, Ghana, Guinea, Guinea-Bissau, Mali, Sao Tome and Principe, Senegal, Sierra Leone, Togo and Uganda.

36   ILO, *Activities in Africa*, p. 41.

37   K. Cowan-Louw, M. Diepart and M. Haour-Knipe, *HIV/AIDS Prevention and Care Programmes for Mobile Populations in Africa: An Inventory* (Geneva: IOM, 2002).

38   http://www.ghana.co.uk/news/content.asp?articleID=9351

39   Tacoli, "Changing Rural-Urban Interactions," p. 19.

40   D. Ratha, "Workers' Remittances: An Important and Stable Source of Development Finance" in *Global Development Finance: Striving for Stability in Development Finance* (Washington, DC: World Bank, 2003), p. 157.

41   IOM, *World Migration Report 2003*, p. 230.

42   D. Kapur, "Remittances: The New Development Mantra?" G-24 Technical Group Meeting, 2003, p. 6

43   C. Sander, *Migrant Remittances to Developing Countries: A Scoping Study* (London: DFID, 2003), p. 15

44   See http://www1.umn.edu/humanrts/instree/z2arcon.htm

45   O. Bakewell, "Refugee Aid and Protection in Rural Africa" New Issues in Refugee Research No. 35. Geneva: UNHCR, 2001.

46   A. De Haan, "Migrants, Livelihoods and Rights: The Relevance of Migration in Development Policies" Social Development Working Paper No. 4, DFID, London, 2000, p. 17.

47   UN, *International Migration 2002 Wallchart*.

48   J. Arthur, "International Labor Migration Patterns in West Africa" *African Studies Review* 34(3) (1991).

49   B. Kalasa, *West Africa Long Term Perspective Study: Settlement Patterns in West Africa* (Paris: OECD Sahel and West Africa Club, 1994), p. 23.

50   *Ibid.*, p. 14. Nigeria is excluded primarily because of the poor quality of its population statistics.

51   N. Robin, *Atlas des migrations ouest-africaines vers l'Europe, 1985-1993* (Paris: Editions Orstom, 1997).

52   A. Ba, Undeterred: Seeking Succor far from Home, *Dollars & Sense*, Baruch College. 2003.

53   M. Diatta and N. Mbow, "Releasing the Development Potential of Return Migration: The Case of Senegal" *International Migration* 37(1) (1999): 243-64.

54   Kapur, Remittances: The New Development Mantra? p. 23.

55   J. Toto, "West African Immigration and Cross-Border Interpersonal Transfers in Côte d'Ivoire: Lessons from a Real Economy in Darkness" Paper presented at International Workshop on Migration and Poverty in West Africa, Sussex Centre for Migration Research, University of Sussex, 2003.

56   Diatta and Mbow, "Releasing the Development Potential of Return Migration."

57   J. van Doorn, "Migration, Remittances and Development." *Labour Education* 129(4) (2002), p. 51.

58   See http://www.house.gov/lantos/caucus/TestimonyStacy052103.htm

59   S. Traoré and P. Bocquier, Synthèse régionale, réseau migration et urbanisation en Afrique de l'Ouest (REMUAO). Études et Travaux du CERPOD. Bamako, CERPOD. 15, 1998.

60   S. Findley, "Migration and Family Interactions in Africa" in A. Adepoju, (ed.), *Family, Population and Development in Africa* (London: Zed Books, 1998).

61   Representative surveys were conducted in Burkina Faso, Côte d'Ivoire, Guinea, Mali, Mauritania, Niger, Senegal and Nigeria; see Traoré and Bocquier, "Synthese regionale."

62   S. Findley, "Does Drought Increase Migration? Study of Migration from Rural Mali during the 1983-1985 Drought" *International Migration Review* 28(3) (1994): 539-53.

63   See http://www.fao.org/DOCREP/004/X6543E/X6543E03.htm

64   See http://www.afrol.com/News2001/afr027_human_trafficking.htm

65   See http://allafrica.com/stories/200305210167.html

66   Conflict and Development Policy in the Mano River Region and Côte d'Ivoire: The Regional Stakes for Stability and Reconstruction (Paris: OECD, 2003).

67   See http://www.usembassy.it/file2001_12/alia/a1122702.htm

68   UNICEF, *Child Trafficking in West Africa: Policy Responses* (Florence: UNICEF Innocenti Research Centre, 2002).

69   Interview with Nikhil Roy, Anti-Slavery International, 12 February 2004.

70   S. Castle and A. Diarra, "The International Migration of Young Malians: Tradition, Necessity or Rite of Passage?" London, London School of Hygiene and Tropical Medicine, 2003.

71   R. Grillo and B. Riccio, "Translocal Development: Italy-Senegal" Paper for International Workshop on Migration and Poverty in West Africa, Sussex Centre for Migration Research, University of Sussex, 2003.

72   P. Stoller, "Marketing Afrocentricity: West African Trade Networks in North America" in K. Koser (ed.), *New African Diasporas* (London: Routledge, 2003), pp. 93-123.

73   See IOM and IMP, "Report and Conclusions from the International Migration Policy Seminar for West Africa," Dakar, 2001.

74   Diatta and Mbow, "Releasing the Development Potential of Return Migration."

75   Arthur, "International Labor Migration Patterns in West Africa," p. 74.

76   K. Meagher, "Shifting the Imbalance: The Impact of Structural Adjustment on Rural-Urban Population Movements in Northern Nigeria" *Journal of Asian and African Studies* 22(1997), p. 83.

77   World Bank, *Nigeria: Poverty in the Midst of Plenty* (Washington DC: World Bank, 1997), p. 106.

78   C. Ekpunobi, "Migration into Abuja: Environmental Effects." *Daily Trust* (Abuja) 2003.

79   O. Ibeanu, "Exiles in their Own Home: Conflicts and Internal Population Displacement in Nigeria." *Journal of Refugee Studies* 12(2) (1999), p. 168.

80   S. Anyanwu, "Spatial Population Maldistribution in Nigeria: Causes and Suggestions." *Journal of Development Alternatives and Area Studies* 15(1) (1996), p. 26.

81   Meagher, "Shifting the Imbalance," p. 88.

82   World Bank *Nigeria*, p. vii.

83   Tacoli, "Changing Rural-Urban Interactions," p. 22.

84   A. Adebayo, "Contemporary Dimensions of Migration among Historically Migrant Nigerians: Fulani Pastoralists in Southwestern Nigeria" *Journal of Asian and African Studies* 32 (1997).

85   M. Hollos, "Migration, Education, and the Status of Women in Southern Nigeria." *American Anthropologist* 93(4) (1991).

86   See http://allafrica.com/stories/200201220075.html

87   USDOS, *Trafficking in Persons Report: Trafficking Victims Protection Act of 2000* (Washington: United States Department of State, 2003).

88   See http://www.africa.upenn.edu/Urgent_Action/apic020303.html

89   IOM, *World Migration Report 2003*, p. 216.

90   R. Adams, "International Migration, Remittances and the Brain Drain" World Bank Policy Research Working Paper 3069 (2003).

91   IOM, *World Migration Report 2003*, p. 219.

92   R. Blench, "Position Paper on Migration" DFID, London, 2004, p. 7.

93   I. Jumare, "The Displacement of the Nigerian Academic Community" *Journal of Asian and African Studies* 32 (1997), p. 117.

94   R. Reynolds, "An African Brain Drain: Igbo Decisions to Emigrate to the US" *Review of African Political Economy* 29 (2002).

95   Blench, "Position Paper on Migration," p. 7.

96   U. Osili, "Remittances from International Migration: An Empirical Investigation using a Matched Sample" Department of Economics, Indiana University - Purdue University, Indianapolis, 2001.

97   Blench, "Position Paper on Migration," p. 7.

98   C.-E.Chikezie, "The African Diaspora: Prototype Pan-Africanists or Parochial Village-aiders?" Draft discussion paper for African Knowledge Networks Forum (AKNF) Meeting, Addis Ababa, October 2001.

99   See http://www.digitalpartners.org/news_files/diasporas.html

100   See http://search.csmonitor.com/durable/2001/02/26/fp7s1-csm.shtml

101   A listing of Nigerian associations abroad is provided on Nigeria Info Net, http://www.nigeriainfonet.com/

102   USDOS, *Trafficking in Persons*.

103   *Ibid.*

104   Anyanwu, "Spatial Population Maldistribution in Nigeria," pp. 27-29.

105   C. Obgeh, "Why Nigeria's Economy is in Trouble" *This Day* 4 November 2003.

106   Blench, "Position Paper on Migration," p. 14.

107   Ibeanu, "Exiles in their Own Home," p. 176.

108   Data from http://www.unhcr.ch

109   J. Litchfield and H. Waddington, "Migration and Poverty in Ghana: Evidence from the Ghana Living Standards Survey" Centre for Migration Research, University of Sussex, 2003.

110   J. Anarfi, J. S. Kwankye, O. Ababio and R. Tiemoko, "Migration from and to Ghana: A Background Paper" Development Research Centre on Migration, Globalisation and Poverty, Sussex University, 2004.

111   H. Coulombe and S. Canagarajah, "Employment, Labor Markets and Poverty in Ghana: A Study of Changes during Economic Decline and Recovery" Working Paper, World Bank.

112   D. Cleveland, "Migration in West Africa: A Savanna Village Perspective" *Africa* 61(2) (1991): 222-46.

113   E. Kunfaa, "Consultations with the Poor: Ghana Synthesis Report" Report commissioned by the World Bank, Centre for Development of People (CEDEP), Kumasi.

114   A. Mensah-Bonsu, *Migration and Environmental Pressure in Northern Ghana* (Amsterdam: Vrije Universiteit, 2003).

115   *Ibid.*

116   Litchfield and Waddington, "Migration and Poverty in Ghana."

117   Cleveland, "Migration in West Africa."

118   Mensah-Bonsu, Migration and Environmental Pressure.

119   J. Anarfi, "Sexuality, Migration and AIDS in Ghana: A Socio-Behavioural Study" *Health Transition Review* 3(1993): 45-67.

120   L. Brydon, "Ghanaian Women in the Migration Process" in S. Chant (ed.), *Gender and Migration in Developing Countries*, London and New York: Bellhaven Press, 1992, p. 96.

121   ILO/IPEC, *Combating Trafficking in Children for Labour Exploitation in West and Central Africa* (Geneva: ILO, 2001), p. 37.

122   Data from EUROSTAT.

123   R. Black, R. Tiemoko and C. Waddington, "International Migration, Remittances and Poverty: The Case of Ghana and Côte d'Ivoire," Sussex Centre for Migration Research Paper prepared for the World Bank. Brighton: University of Sussex.

124   N. Van Hear, *New Diasporas: The Mass Exodus, Dispersal and Regrouping of Migrant Communities* (London, UCL Press, 1998).

125   *Ibid.*

126   A. Asiedu, "Some Benefits of Migrants' Return Visits to Ghana" Presented at International Workshop on Migration and Poverty in West Africa," University of Sussex, Brighton, 2003.

127   See http://www.myjoyonline.com/frontarts.asp?p=3&a=7340

128   Black, Tiemoko and Waddington, "International Migration, Remittances and Poverty."

129   N. Nuro, "Brain Drain from Ghana: Case of University Lecturers," Department of Geography and Tourism, University of Cape Coast, 1999.

130   http://www.ghanaian-chronicle.com/230501.page2m.htm

131   http://www.myjoyonline.come/frontarts.asp?p=3&a=7649

132   J. Buchan and D. Dovlo, "International Recruitment of Health Workers to the UK: A Report for DFID," Department for International Development, Accra, 2003.

133   R. Black and E. Brusset, "Emergency Relief and Reconstruction: A Study of the Liberian Experience," United Nations, Department of Economic and Social Affairs, New York, 2000.

134   See R. Fanthorpe, "Locating the Politics of a Sierra Leonean Chiefdom" *Africa* 68(4) (1998): 558-83.

135   UNDP, *Human Development Report 2003* (New York: UNDP, 2003).

136   T. Makannah, "Remittances and Rural Development in Sierra Leone" *Peasant Studies* 16(1) (1988): 53-62.

137   Amco-Robertson Mineral Services Ltd., "Sierra Leone Diamond Policy Study," Department for International Development, Freetown, 2002.

138   Makannah, "Remittances and Rural Development," p. 58.

139   *Ibid.*, pp. 55-6.

140   D. Frost, "Diasporan West African Communities: The Kru in Freetown and Liverpool" *Review of African Political Economy* 92 (2002): 285-300.

141   Republic of Sierra Leone, *Interim Poverty Reduction Strategy Paper.* Freetown, Republic of Sierra Leone, 2001.

142   See http://www.uniqueservers.net/vision2025/

143   See http://www.sieraleonehomecoming.com

144   USDOS, *Trafficking in Persons Report.*

145   See http://allafrica.com/stories/200402050575.html

146   de Haan, "Migrants, Livelihoods and Rights."

147   W. Gould, "Circulation and Schooling in East Africa" in M. Prothero and M. Chapman (eds.), *Circulation in Third World Countries* (London: Routledge, 1985), pp. 262-78.

148   J. Oucho, "Emigration Dynamics of Eastern African Countries" *International Migration* 33 (1995): 391-434.

149   W. Gould, "Regional Labour Migration Systems in East Africa: Continuity and Change" in R. Cohen (ed.), *Cambridge Survey of World Migration* (Cambridge: Cambridge University Press, 1995), pp. 183-89.

150   Oucho, "Emigration Dynamics."

151   Potts, "Shall We Go Home?"

152   IOM, *World Migration Report 2003,* Chapter 12.

153 E. Francis, "Gender, Migration and Multiple Livelihoods: Cases from Eastern and Southern Africa" *Journal of Development Studies* 38(2002): 167-90.

154 E. Francis, *Making a Living: Changing Livelihoods in Rural Africa* (London: Routledge, 2002).

155 A De Haan with with K. Brock, G. Carswell, N. Coulibaly, H. Seba and K. Toufique, "Migration and Livelihoods: Case Studies in Bangladesh, Ethiopia and Mali" IDS Research Report No. 446, Institute for Development Studies, Sussex University, 2000.

156 R. Goodrich, "Sustainable Rural Livelihoods: A Summary of Research in Mali and Ethiopia" IDS Research Report, Institute for Development Studies. Sussex University, 2001.

157 E. Kebede, "Ethiopia: An Assessment of the International Migration Situation. The Case of Female Labour Migrants" Working Paper No. 3, Gender Promotion Programme, International Labour Office, Geneva, 2001.

158 Sander, "Migrant Remittances to Developing Countries."

159 D. Shinn, "Reversing the Brain Drain in Ethiopia" Addis Tribune 2002.

160 IOM, *World Migration Report 2003*, Chapter 12.

161 Chapter 28, Article 164 COMESA Treaty, 1994; http://www.comesa.int/about/treaty/treaty_pdf

162 "African Development Bank Loan for Tackling Massive Migration Problem" *IRIN* 20 October 2003.

163 J. Mwamunyange, "Fears over Jobs as Customs Union Looms" The East African 27 October 2003.

164 African NGOs Refugee Protection Network, "Overview of Workshop on Protecting Refugee Rights in East Africa: The Need for a Progressive Legislative and Policy Framework, April 19-20, 2002," Mombasa, Kenya.

165 "Great Lakes: Region Recommits to Refugee Protection, Undecided on Burden Sharing" IRIN 19 September 2003.

166 K. Okoth, "Kenya: What Role for Diaspora in Development" Migration Policy Institute, Washington, 2003.

167 Data from http://www.unhcr.ch

168 See http://www.db.idpproject.org/Sites/IdpProjectDb/idpSurvey.nsf/wViewSingleEnv/KenyaProfile+Summary

169 A. Bigsten, "The Circular Migration of Smallholders in Kenya" *Journal of African Economies* 5(1996): 1-20.

170 R. Oniang'o "The Impact of Out-Migration on Household Livelihoods and on the Management of Natural Resources: A Kenyan Case Study" *IDS Bulletin* 6(1996): 54-60.

171 J. Nelson, "Makueni District Profile: Income Diversification and Farm Investment, 1989-1999," Drylands Research, Crewcorne, Somerset, 2002.

172 Oniang'o, "Impact of Out-Migration."

173   R. Agesa, *Migration and Gender Wage Differences in Kenya* (Milwaukee: University of Wisconsin, 1996).

174   J. Agesa and R. Agesa, "Gender Differences in the Incidence of Rural to Urban Migration: Evidence from Kenya" *Journal of Development Studies* 35(1999): 36-58.

175   J. Hoddinott, "A Model of Migration and Remittances Applied to Western Kenya" *Oxford Economic Papers* 46(1994): 459-76.

176   J. Oucho, *Urban Migrants and Rural Development in Kenya* (Nairobi: Nairobi University Press, 1996).

177   USDOS, *Trafficking in Persons Report.*

178   C. Sander, "Capturing a Market Share? Migrant Remittance Transfers and Commercialiisation of Microfinance in Africa" Paper for Conference on Current Issues in Microfinance, Johannesburg, 12-14 August 2003.

179   De Haan, "Migrants, Livelihoods and Rights," p. 17.

180   K. Kabbucho, C. Sander and P. Mukwana, "Passing the Buck. Money Transfer Systems: The Practice and Potential for Products in Kenya," MicroSave-Africa, Nairobi, 2003.

181   S. Bach, "International Migration of Health Workers: Labour and Social Issues," Sectoral Activities Programme Working Paper, International Labour Office, Geneva, 2003.

182   T. Stokes, "Kenya's Brain Drain" *Daily Nation* 8 March 2001.

183   M. Kaul, "Reversing Africa's Brain Drain: The Africa Recruit Initiative and the Challenge to Governments, the Diaspora and the Private Sector," Commonwealth Business Council, London, 2003.

184   Shinn, "Reversing the Brain Drain in Ethiopia."

185   P. Mwaura, "Comment (Gigiri notebook)" *Daily Nation* 29 May 2003.

186   K. Salmon, "Kenya Grapples with Brain Drain Troubles" *Inter Press Service* 2003.

187   Government of Kenya, *Kenya: Interim Poverty Reduction Strategy Paper 2000-2003*, Nairobi, 2002, p. 27.

188   Salmon, "Kenya Grapples with Brain Drain Troubles."

189   Shinn, "Reversing the Brain Drain in Ethiopia."

190   Okoth, "Kenya: What Role for Diaspora in Development."

191   "Kenya Foreign Worker Visas" *BBC Website* 28 October 2003.

192   USDOS, *Trafficking in Persons Report.*

193   http://www.db.idpproject.org/Sites/ldpProjectDb/idpSurvey.nsf/wViewSingleEnv/ KenayProfile+Summary

194   Global IDP Database, "350,000 Internally Displaced People Reported in Kenya," Norwegian Refugee Council, 2003.

195   B. Whitaker, "Changing Opportunities: Refugees and Host Communities in Western Tanzania"

New Issues in Refugee Research No. 11, United Nations High Commissioner for Refugees, Geneva, 1999.

196   Data from http://www.unhcr.ch

197   Many more – perhaps as many as half a million – may have also resettled in local villages; see S. Hoyweghen, "Mobility, Territoriality and Sovereignty in Post-Colonial Tanzania" New Issues in Refugee Research No. 49, United Nations High Commissioner for Refugees, Geneva, 2001.

198   Tacoli, "Changing Rural-Urban Interactions in Sub-Saharan Africa."

199   F. Lerise, "The Case of Himo and its Region, Northern Tanzania" Briefing Paper Series on Rural-Urban Interactions and Livelihood Strategies No. 1, International Institute for Environment and Development, London, 2001.

200   F. Lerise, "The Case of Lindi and its Region, Southern Tanzania" Briefing Paper Series on Rural-Urban Interactions and Livelihood Strategies No. 2, International Institute for Environment and Development, London, 2001.

201   De Haan, "Migrants, Livelihoods and Rights."

202   M. Mbonile, "Migration and Urban Development in Tanzania: Internal Responses to Structural Adjustment" in W. Gould and A. Findlay (eds.), *Population Migration and the Changing World Order* (Chichester: John Wiley and Sons, 1994), pp. 249-72.

203   Sander, "Migrant Remittances to Developing Countries."

204   C. Sander, P. Mukwana and A. Millinga, "Passing the Buck: Money Transfer Systems. The Practice and Potential for Products in Tanzania and Uganda" MicroSave Africa, London, 2003, p. 7.

205   Whitaker, "Refugees and Host Communities in Western Tanzania."

206   USDOS, *Trafficking in Persons Report.*

207   M. Mbonile, "Trading Centre and Development in a Remote Rural District of Tanzania" *Review of African Political Economy* 59 (1994): 7-20.

208   USDOS, *Trafficking in Persons Report.*

209   Hoyweghen, "Mobility, Territoriality and Sovereignty in Post-Colonial Tanzania."

210   Data from http://www.unhcr.ch

211   UN, International Migration Report 2002 (New York: United Nations Department of Economic and Social Affairs, Population Division, 2002); and UN, *World Population Prospects 2000 Revision* (New York: United Nations Department of Economic and Social Affairs, Population Division, 2002).

212   UN, *International Migration Report 2002.*

213   Interview with Michael Wafula, Assistant Commissioner for Refugees, Prime Minister's Office, 9 December 2003.

214   See http://www.idpproject.org/countries/uganda/Uganda.htm

215 See http://www.db.idpproject.org/Sites/idpSurvey.nsf/wViewSingleEnv/ UgandaProfile+Summary

216 *Ibid.*

217 Ratha, "Workers' Remittances" p. 160.

218 UNAAnet, 16 January 2004 Ugandan North America Association (www.unaaboston.com)

219 C. Dolan, "Gender and Diverse Livelihoods in Uganda" UEA LADDER Working Paper No 10, University of East Anglia, Norwich, 2002.

220 A. Nunn, H. Wagner, A. Kamali and J. Kengeya-Kayondo, "Migrations and HIV-1 Seroprevalence in a Rural Ugandan Population" *AIDS* 9 (1995): 503-6.

221 M. Macchiavello, "Forced Migrants as an Under-Utilized Asset: Refugee Skills, Livelihoods, and Achievements in Kampala, Uganda" New Issues in Refugee Research No. 95, UNHCR, Geneva, 2002.

222 Adepoju, "Emigration Dynamics in Sub-Saharan Africa."

223 Adepoju, "Emigration Dynamics in Sub-Saharan Africa."

224 W. Carrington and E. Detragiache, "How Big Is the Brain Drain?" Working Paper, International Monetary Fund, Washington, 1998.

225 E. Kumira and F. Vateganya, "Where Has All the Education Gone in Uganda" Institute for Development Studies and Faculty of Social Science, Makerere University, Brighton and Kampala, 2003.

226 Adepoju, "Emigration Dynamics in Sub-Saharan Africa."

227 UN, *International Migration 2002.*

228 See http://www.unaaboston.com/

229 See http://www.buganda.com/diaspora.htm

230 Ministry of Finance, Planning and Economic Development, *Uganda Poverty Status Report 2003* (Kampala, 2003)

231 See the Rwanda Diaspora Global Network at http://www.rwandadiaspora.org

232 See http://www.rwanda.net

233 M. Ngendakumana, "Migrations dans les pays interlacustres: cas du Ruanda et du Burundi" Famille, Santé, *Developpement / Imbonezamuryango* 21(1991): 10-19.

234 UN, *International Migration 2002* suggests an average net emigration of 343,000 each year from 1990-95, and a net immigration of 395,000 from 1996-2000. However, this reflects the departure of an estimated 1.7 million after the genocide in 1994, the return of an estimated 800,000 'old caseload' refugees from 1959 onwards who returned at that time, and the gradually return of 'new caseload' refugees from 1995 onwards.

235 *Ibid.*

236 Data from http://www.unhcr.ch

237   Ministry of Finance and Economic Planning, Enquête integrale sur les conditions de vie des ménages au Rwanda: 2000-2001 (Kigali, 2002).

238   See http://www.db.idpproject.org/Sites/IdpprojectDb/idpSurvey.nsf/wCountries/Rwanda

239   USDOS, *Trafficking in Persons Report*.

240   World Food Programme, "Rwanda Food Security Update, Jan-Feb 2004" (Kigali, 2003).

241   Government of Rwanda, *Vision 2020* (Kigali, 1998).

242   An IMF study based on 1990 US census figures suggests just 2.2 per cent of tertiary-educated Rwandans were in the US; see Carrington and Detragiache, "How Big Is the Brain Drain?"

243   D. McDonald (ed.), *On Borders: Perspectives on International Migration in Southern Africa* (Cape Town and New York: SAMP and St Martin's Press, 2000).

244   J. Crush and D. McDonald (eds.), *Transnationalism and New African Immigration to South Africa* (Cape Town and Toronto: SAMP and CAAS, 2002).

245   B. Dodson, *Women on the Move: Gender and Cross-Border Migration to South Africa* (Southern African Migration Project, Migration Policy Series No. 9, 1998).

246   B. Williams, M. Lurie, E. Gouws and J. Crush, *Spaces of Vulnerability: Migration and HIV/AIDS in South Africa* (Southern African Migration Project, Migration Policy Series No. 24, 2002) and International Organization for Migration, *Mobile Populations and HIV/AIDS in the Southern African Region* (Pretoria: IOM and UNAIDS, 2003).

247   J. Klaaren and B. Rutinwa, *Towards the Harmonization of Immigration and Refugee Law in SADC*, MIDSA Report No. 1, Cape Town, 2004.

248   J. Crush, A. Jeeves and D. Yudelman, *South Africa's Labor Empire: A History of Black Migrancy to the Gold Mines* (Cape Town and Boulder: David Philip and Westview Press, 1992); J. Crush and W. James (eds.), *Crossing Boundaries: Mine Migrancy in a Democratic South Africa* (Cape Town: Idasa Publishing, 1995); and A. Jeeves and J. Crush (eds.), *White Farms, Black Labour: The State and Agrarian Change in Southern Africa* (New York, London and Pietermaritzburg: Heinemann, James Currey and University of Natal Press, 1997).

249   Crush and James, *Crossing Boundaries*.

250   K. Philip, "Job Creation through Rural Enterprise Support: A Case Study of the Mineworkers Development Agency" (http://www.projectliteracy.org.za/tmpl/programme.htm); S. Barton, "Mineworkers Development Agency: Internal Assessment" (http://www.enterprise-impact.org.uk/word-files/MDAcasenotes.doc); NUM, Mineworkers Development Agency: An Overview of the Programme" 10th NUM Congress, April 2000; Placer Dome Western Areas, CARE Project: Helping Retrenched Miners, Families and Communities throughout Southern Africa (http://www.southdeep.co.za); TEBA, Report on TEBA Rural Development Services (http://www.teba.co.za/products_rdev.html).

251   McDonald, *On Borders*, p. 232.

252   J. Oucho, E. Campbell and E. Mukamaambo, *Botswana: Migration Perspectives and Prospects* (Southern African Migration Project, Migration Policy Series No. 19, 2000); B. Frayne and W. Pendleton, *Mobile Namibia: Migration Trends and Attitudes* (Southern African Migration

Project, Migration Policy Series No. 27, 2002); D. Tevera and L. Zinyama, *Zimbabweans Who Move: Perspectives on International Migration in Zimbabwe* (Southern African Migration Project, Migration Policy Series No. 25, 2002); Sechaba Consultants, *The Border Within: The Future of the Lesotho-South African International Boundary* (Southern African Migration Project, Migration Policy Series No. 26, 2002); and H. Simelane and J. Crush, *Swaziland Moves: Perceptions and Patterns of Modern Migration* (Southern African Migration Project, Migration Policy Series No. 32, 2004).

253 C. Rogerson, *Building Skills: Cross-Border Migrants and the South African Construction Industry* (Southern African Migration Project, Migration Policy Series No. 11, 1999); and J. Crush, C. Mather, F. Mathebula and D. Lincoln, *Borderline Farming: Foreign Migrants in the South African Commercial Agriculture* (Southern African Migration Project, Migration Policy Series No. 16, 2000).

254 J. Crush, "The Discourse and Dimensions of Irregularity in Post-Apartheid South Africa" *International Migration* 37(1999): 125-49.

255 J. McGregor, "Violence and Social Change in a Border Economy: War in the Maputo Hinterland, 1984-1992" *Journal of Southern African Studies* 24(1) (1998): 37-60.

256 A. Morris, *Bleakness and Light: Inner-City Transition in Hillbrow, Johannesburg* (Johannesburg: Wits University Press, 1999); and Alan Morris and Antoine Bouillon (eds.), *African Immigration to South Africa: Francophone Migration of the 1990s* (Pretoria: Protea and IFAS, 2001).

257 South African Law Commission, *Trafficking in Persons* (Issue Paper No. 25, 2004).

258 Molo Songololo, *The Trafficking of Children for Purposes of Sexual Exploitation – South Africa* (Cape Town: Creda, 2000); International Organization for Migration, *Trafficking in Women and Children for Sexual Exploitation in Southern Africa* (Pretoria: IOM, 2003).

259 B. Dodson, "Women on the Move: Gender and Cross Border Migration to South Africa from Lesotho, Mozambique and Zimbabawe" in McDonald, *On Borders* pp. 119-150.

260 *Ibid.*; K. Datta, "Gender, Labour Markets and Female Migration in and from Botswana" in D. Simon (ed.), *South Africa in Southern Africa* (Oxford: James Currey, 1998), pp. 206-221.

261 Dodson, "Women on the Move" p. 124.

262 S. Peberdy and C. Rogerson, "Transnationalism and Non-South African Entrepreneurs in South Africa's Small, Medium and Micro-enterprise (SMME) Economy" *Canadian Journal of African Studies* 34(2000): 20-40.

263 S. Peberdy, "Migration and Poverty" SAMP paper for the South African Department of Social Development, 2003; S. Peberdy and J. Oucho, "Migration and Poverty" SAMP Paper for the ACP-EU Parliamentary Committee, Cape Town, 2002; S. Parnell and D. Wooldridge (eds.), "Social capital and Social Inclusion in the City of Johannesburg and the Implications for Urban Government" Paper for the City of Johannesburg, 2001.

264 McDonald, *On Borders*; Oucho, Campbell and Mukamaambo, "Botswana: Migration Perspectives and Prospects"; Tevera and Zinyama, Zimbabweans Who Move; Sechaba Consultants, Poverty and Livelihoods in Lesotho (Maseru, 2002).

265 Genesis, *Supporting Cross-Border Remittances in Southern Africa: Estimating Market Potential and Assessing Regulatory Obstacles* (Johannesburg: Finmark Trust, 2003).

266   *Ibid.*; C Sander, "Migrant Remittances to Developing Countries"; DFID and World Bank. "Report and Conclusions: International Conference on Migrant Remittances: Development Impact, Opportunities for the Financial Sector and Future Prospects," London, October 2003.

267   Sander, "Migrant Remittances to Developing Countries," p. 15.

268   DFID and World Bank, "Report and Conclusions," p. 7; see also R. Adams, "International Migration, Remittances, and the Brain Drain" Paper for the World Bank, Washington, June 2003.

269   *Ibid.*, p. 5.

270   G. B. Frayne, *Survival of the Poorest: Food Security and Migration in Namibia.* PhD Thesis. Kingston: Queen's University, 2001.

271   S. Peberdy and C. Rogerson, "Creating New Spaces? Immigrant Entrepreneurship in South Africa's SMME Economy," in R. Kloosterman and J. Rath (eds.), *Immigrant Entrepreneurs: Venturing Abroad in the Age of Globalization* (Oxford: Berg, 2002); S. Peberdy and J. Crush, "Invisible Travellers, Invisible Trade? Informal Sector Cross Border Trade and the Maputo Corridor Spatial Development Initiative" *South African Geographical Journal* 83 (2001): 115-23; S. Peberdy, "Mobile Entrepreneurship: Informal Cross-Border Trade and Street Trade in South Africa" *Development Southern Africa* 17 (2001): 201-19; S. Peberdy, "Border Crossings: Small Entrepreneurs and Informal Sector Cross Border Trade between South Africa and Mozambique" *Tjidschrift voor Economische en Sociale Geographie* 91 (2000): 361-78; V. Muzvidziwa, "Cross-Border Trade: A Strategy for Climbing Out of Poverty in Masvingo, Zimbabwe" *Zambezia* 25 (1998): 29-58; J. Macamo, "Estimates of Unrecorded Cross-Border Trade between Mozambique and Her Neighbors: Implications for Food Security" Report for the Regional Economic Development Support Office for Eastern and Southern Africa, USAID, 1998; I. Minde and T. Nakhumwa, "Informal Cross-Border Trade between Malawi and Her Neighbouring Countries" Report for the Regional Economic Development Support Office for Eastern and Southern Africa, USAID, 1998.

272   C. Rogerson, *International Migration, Immigrant Entrepreneurs and South Africa's Small Enterprise Economy* (SAMP Migration Policy Series, No. 3, 1998).

273   Peberdy and Rogerson, "Creating New Spaces?"; Peberdy and Crush, "Invisible Travellers, Invisible Trade?"; Peberdy, "Mobile Entrepreneurship."

274   Dodson, "Women on the Move"; B. Dodson, "Discrimination by Default?: Gender Concerns in South African Immigration Policy" *Africa Today* 48(2001): 72-89.

275   Dodson, "Women on the Move" p. 126

276   See Census 2001 at http://www.statssa.gov.za

277   Crush et al, Spaces of Vulnerability; IOM, *Mobile Populations and HIV/AIDS.*

278   H. Bhorat, J-B. Meyer and C. Mlatsheni, Skilled Labour Migration from Developing Countries: Study on South and Southern Africa International Migration Papers No. 52, International Labour Organization, Geneva, 2002.

279   J. Crush, "The Global Raiders: Nationalism, Globalization and the South African Brain Drain" *Journal of International Affairs* 56 (2002): 147-72.

280   J. Xaba and G. Phillips, "Understanding Nurse Emigration: Final Report" Research Report for the Democratic Nursing Organisation of South Africa, Pretoria, 2001.

281   A. Padarath, C. Chamberlain, D. McCoy, A. Ntuli, M. Rowson and R. Loewenson, "Health Personnel in Southern Africa: Confronting Maldistribution and Brain Drain" Equinet Discussion Paper No. 3, Harare, 2003.

282   Ibid.; OECD, *Trends in International Migration: Part 111: The International Mobility of Health Professionals: An Evaluation and Analysis Based on the Case of South Africa* (Paris: OECD, 2003).

283   J. Oucho and J, Crush, "Contra Free Movement: South Africa and SADC Migration Protocols" *Africa Today* 48(3): 139-58.

284   *Ibid.*

285   Klaaren and Rutinwa, *Harmonization of Immigration and Refugee Law.*

286   *Ibid.*

287   J. Klaaren and J. Ramji, "Inside Illegality: Migration Policing in South Africa After Apartheid" *Africa Today* 48 (2001): 35-48.

288   Human Rights Watch, *Prohibited Persons: Abuse of Undocumented Migrants, Asylum-Seekers, and Refugees in South Africa* (New York: Human Rights Watch, 1998); South African Human Rights Commission. "Lindela at the Crossroads for Detention and Repatriation: An Assessment of the Conditions of Detention," South African Human Rights Commission, 2000.

289   Klaaren and Rutinwa, *Harmonization of Immigration and Refugee Law*; J. Crush and C. Tshitereke, "Contesting Migrancy: The Foreign Labor Debate in Post-1994 South Africa" *Africa Today* 48(2002): 49-70.

290   Klaaren and Rutinwa, *Harmonization of Immigration and Refugee Law.*

291   South African Human Rights Commission. "Lindela at the Crossroads."

292   Klaaren and Rutinwa, *Harmonization of Immigration and Refugee Law*; Crush and Tshitereke, "Contesting Migrancy."

293   Klaaren and Rutinwa, *Harmonization of Immigration and Refugee Law.*

294   *Ibid.*

295   *Ibid.*

296   *Ibid.*

297   *Ibid.*

298   *Ibid.*

299   *Ibid.*

300   South African Law Reform Commission, "Trafficking in Persons."

301   International Organization for Migration, *Trafficking in Women and Children for Sexual Exploitation.*

302   For instance, Lawyers for Human Rights, Jesuit Refugee Services, South African Council of Churches.

303   J. Crush and W. Pendleton, Regionalizing Xenophobia? Citizen Attitudes to Immigration and Refugee Policy in Southern Africa (Southern African Migration Project, Migration Policy Series No. 30, 2004).

304   Community Agency for Social Enquiry, National Refugee Baseline Survey: Final Report Report for JICA and the UNHCR, Johannesburg, 2003.

305   SAMP, "Making Up the Numbers: Measuring "Illegal Immigration" to South Africa" SAMP Migration Policy Brief No. 3, 2002.

306   F. de Vletter, "Labour Migration to South Africa: The Lifeblood for Southern Mozambique" in McDonald, On Borders, pp. 46-70.

307   L. Zinyama, "Who, What, When and Why: Cross-Border Movement from Zimbabwe to South Africa" in McDonald, On Borders, pp. 71-85.

308   OECD, Trends in International Migration.

309   T. Martineau, K. Decker and T. Bundred, "Briefing Note on International Migration of Health Professionals: Levelling the Playing Field for Developing Country Health Systems" School of Tropical Medicine, Liverpool University, 2002.

310   Organisation for Economic Cooperation and Development, International Migration of Physicians and Nurses: Causes, Consequences and Health Policy (Paris: OECD, 2002).

311   Department of Health, "Migration of Health Professionals: Recruitment and Retention Strategy" (Pretoria, 2001).

312   Michael Kahn et al, Flight of the Flamingoes: A Study on the Mobility of R & D Workers (Cape Town: HSRC and CSIR, 2004).

313   See http://www.sansa.nrf.ac.za/interface/AboutSANSA.htm

314   S. Reid, "Community Service for Health Professionals" South African Health Review (2002). Durban: Health Systems Trust.

315   Based on W. Chirwa "Demographic and Migration Trends in Malawi" Southern African Migration Project, 2000.

316   Padarath et al, "Health Personnel in Southern Africa."

317   L. Cliggett, "Economic and Social Components of Migration In Two Regions, Southern Province" Institute for International Policy Analysis, Bath, 1997.

318   C.J. Chetsanga, An Analysis of the Cause and Effect of the Brain Drain in Zimbabwe (Harare: Scientific and Industrial Research and Development Centre (SIRDC), 2003), p. 25.

319   Because the SIRDC study does not explain the basis of its sampling procedure or how many responses were actually received, it is not possible to say how representative the reported findings actually are on, for example, the likelihood of return. The results are therefore not reported here.

320   Rudo Gaidzanwa, Voting With Their Feet: Migrant Zimbabwean Nurses and Doctors in the

Era of Structural Adjustment (Nordiska Afrikainstitutet, Uppsala, Research Report No. 111, 1999).

321   *Ibid.*

322   D. Potts, "Urban Unemployment and Migrants in Africa: Evidence from Harare, 1985-94" *Development and Change* 31 (2000): 879-910.

323   D. Ranga, "Sub-Region Differentials in Migration and Remittances in Zimbabwe between 1988-90 and 1996-98" *Eastern African Social Science Research Review* 19(2) (2003).

324   V. Muzvidziwa, "Cross-Border Trade: A Strategy for Climbing Out of Poverty in Masvingo, Zimkbabwe" *Zambezia* 25 (1998).